Steps in history 3

L. F. Hobley

Hutchinson

London   Melbourne   Sydney   Auckland   Johannesburg

Preface

STEPS IN HISTORY is a narrative course in world history for pupils of eleven to fourteen years old. It aims to combine the recreation of historical events with an analysis of the evidence those ages have left behind them.

The first two pages of each topic offer a narrative of events; the second two pages develop the pupil's understanding of the narrative through a developing sequence of questions.

Questions 1–5 are of the same kind for each topic. They offer the simplest kind of comprehension, from which pupils can begin to familiarize themselves with names and basic facts from the text. Questions 3–5 can lead to interesting oral discussion, when pupils can follow up and justify their own written assessment of the relative importance of the given facts.

The later questions are designed to develop the pupil's ability to evaluate evidence, to reason about events, to gain a sense of time sequence, and to take an interest in the influence of events in the past upon the world today. Many of these questions will provide subjects for group and class discussion, while others will encourage pupils to write imaginatively about various subjects and situations.

Acknowledgements

Photographs
The John Hillelson Agency 4, 77, 93, 95; US Embassy 5; The British Museum 8; The Library of Congress 9, 68; The Museum of Rural Life 10, 11; The Mansell Collection 13, 17, 22, 36, 37, 42, 50, 53, 74; Ikon 5, 12, 23, 25, 27, 29, 30, 31, 33, 35, 39, 40, 41, 43, 45, 47, 49, 51, 53, 55, 57, 59, 67, 68, 70, 72, 73, 76, 84, 91, 95; The Post Office 13; Radio Times Hulton Picture Library 14, 40, 41, 75; Leicester Museum 15; Brighton Museum 17; Victoria & Albert Museum 18; Robert Wheeler 19, 78; Museum der Stadt Wien 23; National Library of Austria 23; Barnaby's Picture Library 24; Horniman Museum 27; Freer Gallery of Art 31; India Office Library 32, 33, 35; Michael Holford 34; Camera Press 38, 70; Mary Evans Picture Library 40, 41, 46; New York Historical Society 40, 51; British Library 43; National Library of Australia 45; Arthur Lockwood 44, 67, 69, 89; State Library of Australia 43; State Library of NSW, Australia 43; Picturepoint 47; Royal Commonwealth Society 49; Vicker Limited 49; Roger Viollet 54; Bridgeman Art Library 57, 86; Stanley Gibbons 56, 84, 85; Imperial War Museum 56, 70, 73; Novosti Press Agency 60, 61; John Frost 63, 65, 85, 91; Popperfoto 64, 66, 82; Punch Publications 64.

Illustrations
Kathleen King for all the maps; Robert Wheeler for pp. 6, 7, 14, 81.

Hutchinson & Co. (Publishers) Ltd

An imprint of the Hutchinson Publishing Group

17-21 Conway Street, London W1P 6JD

Hutchinson Publishing Group (Australia) Pty Ltd
PO Box 496, 16-22 Church Street,
Hawthorne, Melbourne, Victoria 3122

Hutchinson Group (NZ) Ltd
32-34 View Road, PO Box 40-086, Glenfield, Auckland 10

Hutchinson Group (SA) (Pty) Ltd
PO Box 337, Bergvlei 2012, South Africa

First published 1983
© L. F. Hobley 1983
Reprinted 1984

Set in Baskerville

Printed and bound in Great Britain by
Anchor Brendon Limited, Tiptree, Essex

British Library Cataloguing in Publication Data
Hobley, L. F.
    Steps in history.
    Vol. 3
    1. World history
    I. Title
    900   D21
ISBN 0 09 151991 8

Design: Robert Wheeler
Picture research: Christine Vincent
Additional material: James M. Hagerty

Contents

1 The modern world

The Middle Ages

It is commonly believed that the Middle Ages ended towards the close of the fifteenth century. The fall of Constantinople in 1453 led to the final flight of the scholars of that city to western Europe, and this, helped by the invention of printing, led to a rapid spread of new ideas, and a new interest in science and exploration. In 1492 America was discovered, and in 1497–8 the voyage of Vasco da Gama opened up the sea-ways to India and the Far East. In the early sixteenth century the complaints about the leaders of the Christian church were brought to a head by Martin Luther, who broke the influence of the Pope and the Catholic church on the way in which the people of western Europe thought about religion. This was known as the Reformation.

Was it to become a European world?

Over the next two and half centuries, these new ideas and discoveries led the European peoples to complete the exploration of most of the rest of the world. They had three main objects: (1) to increase trade, (2) to settle in lands where the climate was suitable, (3) to convert the other peoples to Christianity. Sometimes they killed or drove out the native peoples, sometimes they made them slaves, and sometimes they made peaceful trading agreements with them.

They set up trading stations or settlements where they could make permanent homes for themselves. These grew into large colonial

Modern and traditional teaching methods in a Nigerian school. Poor countries rely on the technology of richer nations.

empires in many parts of the world. The western Europeans were thus spreading their power over many other peoples, while their ideas spread even further. It appeared that the whole world was coming under European control.

For a long time, however, there was little change in the life of the majority of the people of Europe. Most of them lived in villages, and worked on the land, using the same tools and methods which had been used for centuries. Travel was slow, roads were poor, and vehicles were clumsy and uncomfortable. The really modern age did not come until the new ideas were applied to raising crops and making goods by machine instead of by hand.

The use of scientific knowledge in food production, manufacturing and transport, in medicine and control of disease, transformed the life of the mass of the people, first in Britain and other parts of western Europe, and then gradually in other countries in most parts of the world. The population of the world grew steadily, and created the need for more food, clothing and other goods, and this led to the development of better methods of farming, and new ways of weaving cloth and making iron and steel. These processes needed larger, heavier machines, and new sources of power to drive them were developed: water, steam, oil, electricity and nuclear power. Thus the nature of the work began to change as people spent more time watching over machines and less time using their hands.

Trade and transport

Trade increased as population grew, and more and more materials were needed from distant parts of the world, so new methods of transport were developed, and new means of communication followed. News of events which in 1776 took several weeks to travel to the other side of the world, today takes a few seconds, and journeys which then took several weeks now take a few hours. But despite all the progress, the modern world has not yet solved all its problems; in fact it has become a more dangerous world, because many of the things which modern science has made possible are used to destroy people, rather than to help them. The first use of nuclear energy was to make atomic bombs, one of which killed one hundred thousand people outright, and condemned thousands of others to a long, lingering death. These matters are not a question of science, but of politics, and depend on the relationships between countries.

A new force

When the colonies in North America gained their independence from Britain in 1776, and so formed the United States of America, a great new force had come into the world. Before long, other colonies too began to claim independence, and over the next two centuries a large number of new independent countries came into existence. For a long time colonization went on, and much of Asia and almost the whole of Africa was shared out between the British, French, Belgian, Portuguese, Spanish, Dutch and German empires, and it was not until the middle of the twentieth century that most of these had gained their freedom. Most of their people remained very poor. The USA, however, has become one of today's two super powers,

Men on the moon – the major scientific achievement of the 1960s. US astronauts carry out experiments.

and shares the world leadership with the Soviet Union of Russia.

A united world?

As science was applied to methods of warfare, wars became more widespread and more destructive, and the twentieth century has already seen two world wars. This has led to attempts to work out some kind of world organization which could aim at settling matters in a peaceful way, instead of going to war. After the First World War, 1914–18, the League of Nations was formed, and most of the independent countries were members, but it did not stop the Second World War, 1939–45. After that, the United Nations was formed, and again nearly all the countries of the world are members, but how effective it will be remains to be seen. One of the great questions of today is, 'Will there be a Third World War?'

Africa   Latin America   N. America   USSR

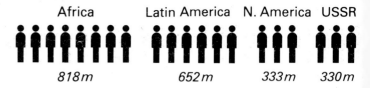

818m   652m   333m   330m

Exercises and things to do

1 Write out, filling in the blanks. One – stands for each missing letter.

The Middle Ages ended during the – – – – – – – – century. There was a new interest in – – – – – – – and in – – – – – – – – – – –. In 1492 – – – – – – – was discovered. There were great changes in – – – – – – – –, and Martin – – – – – – broke away from the – – – – – – – church, and started the – – – – – – – – – –.

New ways of farming, travelling and making things were – – – – – – – – –, and this changed the ways in which people – – – – – and – – – – – –.

The people of – – – – – – explored the rest of the world. They increased – – – – – and took much of the land to – – – – – – in, and so formed great – – – – – – – –. Then the people of the colonies gained their – – – – – – – and became – – – – – – – – – – countries.

New ways of farming, travelling and making things were – – – – – – – – –, and this changed the ways in which people – – – – – and – – – – – –.

2 The heads and tails of these statements have been mixed. Write them out correctly.

(a) Vasco da Gama	(1) started the Reformation in religion.
(b) The League of Nations	(2) was formed after the Second World War.
(c) The USA	(3) is known as the Soviet Union.
(d) The United Nations	(4) was the first attempt to get all countries to work together.
(e) Martin Luther	(5) opened up a sea route to India.
(f) Russia	(6) was once made up of British colonies.

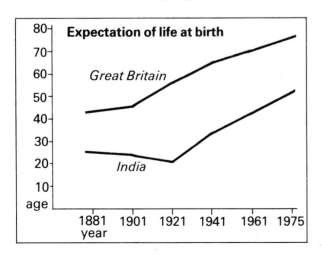

Expectation of life at birth

Great Britain

India

age / year: 1881 1901 1921 1941 1961 1975 (80, 70, 60, 50, 40, 30, 20, 10)

Percentage of the population living towns in Great Britain

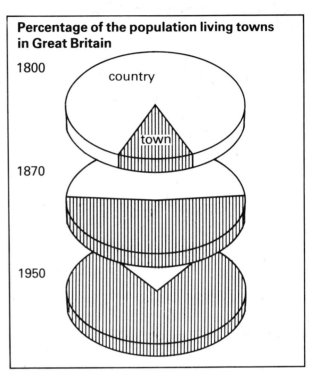

1800   country   town

1870

1950

3 *Statements of fact* Write out the four statements in each group in what you think is their order of importance or interest. Say in each group why you decided to put one particular statement first.

(a) The Middle Ages are considered to have ended in the fifteenth century because
  (1) America was discovered.
  (2) scholars fled from Constantinople.
  (3) printing had been invented.
  (4) people began to understand science.

(b) The European peoples
  (1) explored most of the world.
  (2) settled in many lands.
  (3) increased trade.
  (4) converted many people to Christianity.

(c) The new knowledge of science led to
  (1) an increase in population.
  (2) the use of machines.
  (3) more deadly methods of warfare.
  (4) better means of communication.

4 *The right order* Write these out in the order in which they happened.

(a) The UNO was formed.
(b) The League of Nations was formed.
(c) The American colonies gained their independence.

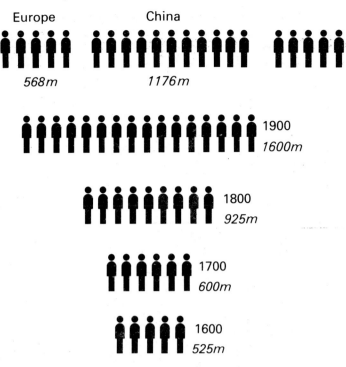

Europe

568m

China

1176m

Asia and Oceania

2602m

Estimated world population in A.D. 2000: *6514m*

1900
1600m

1800
925m

1700
600m

1600
525m

World population growth 1600–2000

5 *The main idea* Write out the one sentence which tells what you think is the main idea of this topic.

(a) The Europeans conquered most of the world, and then lost it again.
(b) Science has changed the life of most people.
(c) Science has not on the whole made life more peaceful.
(d) Man has gained increasing control over nature.
(e) History is a long story of problems to be solved, with new ones arising as old ones are settled.

New York–London communications

1800	Messenger 35 days (written message)	
1858	Morse telegraph Instantaneous (coded message)	
1905	Radio telephone Instantaneous (voice)	
1961	Television satellite Instantaneous (voice and picture)	

6 Study the graph and population figures on this page and answer the following questions:

(a) Which areas in the world today have (i) the smallest and (ii) the largest populations?
(b) Do more or less British people live in towns now than in 1800?
(c) Why do people live longer now than they did in previous centuries?
(d) Why do people in Britain live longer than people in India?

7 Draw posters advertising any two of the Atlantic crossings shown on this page. Mention the date, time taken, destination, price, comfort, etc.

8 List the ways in which you could contact your friends or relatives in the USA (a) in 1800 and (b) today.

9 Explain how machines affect our everyday lives (clues: in the house, transport, offices, hospitals).

10 Read Chapter 22. How do you think man's great scientific achievements can be used to solve problems on earth?

11 Bearing in mind the fact that some people think it is a waste of money, write out arguments for and against space exploration.

12 Using library books to help you, write short biographies of Yuri Gagarin and Neal Armstrong.

Crossing the Atlantic

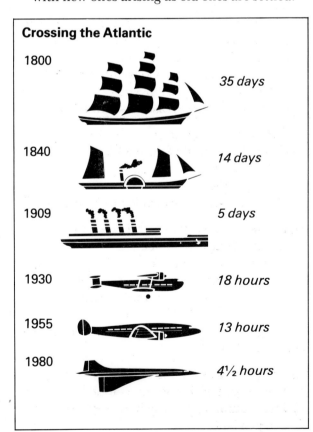

1800 — *35 days*
1840 — *14 days*
1909 — *5 days*
1930 — *18 hours*
1955 — *13 hours*
1980 — *4½ hours*

2 New ways of thinking, new ways of farming

Today thousands of scientists all over the world are constantly working out new ideas, and thousands of engineers and technicians are using these ideas to invent new substances, new processes and new machines. As soon as something is discovered or invented in one country, news of it spreads rapidly throughout almost all the world, and the new ways of doing things quickly bring changes in the way people live and work.

The old ways

In the past things were very different: people scarcely changed their ideas and their ways of thinking, working and living at all. People believed that good and bad harvests, earthquakes, floods, fires, plague, sickness and good health were all due to the anger or the mercy of God, or of evil spirits, or to magic and to miracles. So they did not try to find out the natural causes of events, but attempted to cure their ills by magic and spells.

During much of the Middle Ages, and for many years after that, for century after century people grew the same crops, by the same methods in the same fields, using the same simple tools. They spun their thread and wove their cloth on the same hand spinning wheels and looms in their own homes.

Change

In the seventeenth century some people began to experiment, and to study the world in a scientific way. In the eighteenth century the new ideas began to be put into practice, and so changed the life of the ordinary people. The Royal Society of London for Improving Natural Knowledge was founded in 1662. Chemistry, astronomy, mathematics, botany, physics and the working of the human body were studied. Sir Isaac Newton, (1642–1727) was the greatest English scholar of the time; others from various European countries came to the society's meetings, and put forward their ideas, and described their inventions. Telescopes, microscopes, barometers, thermometers, watches and clocks were invented or improved.

The new knowledge grew very slowly. Most of the leaders of the churches thought it was wrong to question the ways of God and nature, but gradually it began to affect the life of the people. Doctors studied diseases, and were able to prevent many deaths, with the result that the population began to increase quite quickly, and the need for more food encouraged farmers to try out new crops, and new ways of growing the old ones.

The old way of farming

In most villages the old way was to divide the land round the village into three sections. On two of these, wheat or rye, barley, oats, peas and beans were grown. The other was left fallow, that is, without a crop at all, to give the land a rest. The next year another section would be left fallow. This was known as the three field system.

In some villages the three fields were divided up into many long narrow strips, and most of the villagers had several strips on which to grow their own food. With strip farming, the yield was poor, and much land was wasted. There was common grazing ground for all the village cattle and sheep, but the animals were poor in size and quality, and many were killed off in winter.

For most of the villagers life was hard, and many only managed to survive by spinning wool and weaving cloth in their own homes, where all the family, including quite young children had to help.

Most villages and small towns grew practically all the food they needed, and for centuries there had been nothing to encourage them to change the old methods of farming, but in the eighteenth century some towns were growing too large to grow all their own food, and it became profitable for the village folk round about to grow more, and sell it to the townspeople.

'Chemical Lectures' – an etching by Thomas Rowlandson (1810). Such lectures were also regarded as social occasions.

Seed drill

Horse hoe

The new way of farming

The possibility of profitable trade in foodstuffs encouraged some gentlemen farmers to experiment with new crops and new methods, and they began to grow clover and turnips, which provided fodder for sheep and cattle, and at the same time improved the soil. It was found that after growing clover, a field produced a better crop of wheat. It was therefore no longer necessary to leave any land fallow or to kill off the cattle in winter.

Lord Townshend (1674–1738) known as 'Turnip Townshend' because he was very keen on growing turnips, used what is known as the Norfolk four course rotation of crops: one year a field would be sown with clover, the second year with wheat, the third with turnips and the fourth with barley. Then the rotation would start again. This system gave fine harvests.

Jethro Tull (1664–1741) improved the plough so that it would plough more deeply and invented a seed drill, a machine for sowing seeds in rows or drills. He used a horse-drawn hoe to weed between the rows and keep the soil open and cultivated. The new and better fodder, and new methods of animal breeding, led to much larger and meatier cattle and sheep. By 1795 the average sheep sold at Smithfield market was almost three times heavier than it had been in 1710.

Enclosures; the end of strip farming

The old system of dividing up the fields into small narrow strips was not suitable for the use of the seed drill, the horse hoe and other machines. It was clear that good profits could be made from the new farming. Lords of the manor, by this time usually called the squire, were able to ask Parliament to pass Enclosure Acts. These enabled the squire and a few other richer farmers to enclose most of the village farm land into private farms.

The strip fields and common grazing land were divided out among all who had claims to any land, so that each had one plot, which he had to drain and fence or hedge. Many of the villagers could not afford to drain and fence their share, so they sold it to larger landowners, but they usually got very little for it. Some could not prove that they had any claim, so they lost the right to a share in the land they had farmed for years, and so lost everything. They felt that Parliament had robbed them of their land and their rights. They wandered from place to place looking for work, but there were many of them, so wages were very low. Some went to the new factories which were being built in large numbers.

Mechanized harvesting on the American prairie (1891). Horses were still needed to pull the machines.

Exercises and things to do

1 Write out, filling in the blanks. One – stands for each missing letter.

In the seventeenth century the study of science became important, and the $-----$ $-------$ of London for Improving $-------$ $---------$ was founded, in the year $----$. Sir $-----$ $------$ was the greatest English scholar. Doctors improved their understanding of $--------$, and the population $---------$. New ways of farming were $----$ by $----$ $----------$ and $------$ $----$. The big open fields were divided into $-------$ $-----$, and many villagers lost their $-----$ of the land. Life in the villages continued to be very $----$.

2 The heads and tails of these statements have been mixed. Write them out correctly.

(a) Isaac Newton   (1) invented a seed sowing machine.

(b) The three field system   (2) put an end to the old way of farming.

(c) Lord Townshend   (3) was a great English scientist.

(d) Jethro Tull   (4) grew turnips and clover.

(e) An Enclosure Act   (5) shared out the land between all the villagers.

New and better fodder and better methods of breeding led to bigger and bigger animals. In 1797, this pig was eight feet long, nine feet round, and weighed fifty-seven stones.

3 *Statements of fact* Write out the four statements in each group in what you think is their order of importance or interest. Say in each group why you decided to put one particular statement first.

(a) The Royal Society of London for Improving Natural Knowledge
  (1) was founded in 1662.
  (2) held meetings of British and foreign scientists.
  (3) studied various branches of science.
  (4) encouraged great advances in science from 1662 onwards.

(b) Under the old system of farming
  (1) the land was usually divided into three fields, of which one was left fallow.
  (2) most villagers had a share in the village fields which were divided into narrow strips.
  (3) there was much waste of land because each year one field was not used.
  (4) each year the land was divided among the villagers in narrow strips on which they grew their own food.

(c) The new way of farming
  (1) was carried out on private enclosed fields made from the village open fields.
  (2) produced more and better food by using new crops and machines.
  (3) brought profit to richer farmers through better crops, but deprived most villagers of their land.
  (4) left most villagers with no land, so they had to work for wages, which were often very low.

4 *The right order* Write these out in the order in which they happened.

(a) Most land was made into private farms.
(b) The Royal Society of London was formed.
(c) There was little idea of scientific farming.
(d) Tull invented the seed drill.

5 *The main idea* Write out the one sentence which tells what you think is the main idea of this topic.

(a) New ideas in science led to great changes in farming and medicine.
(b) Improved study of medicine led to growth of population.
(c) The Royal Society of London increased our understanding of nature.
(d) Lord Townshend turned his poor land into fertile farms by growing a rotation of crops.

An eight horse-power steam engine and a threshing machine. Despite mechanization a large number of workers were still needed.

6 Look at the graph and population figures on pages 6 and 7. Why do you think it was necessary to produce more food in the nineteenth century?

7 Study the picture of the threshing machine and complete the chart, using the list which follows.

Letter	Activity feature
A	
B	
C	
D	
E	
F	
G	
H	
I	

The feeder man
Man on stack pitching sheaves
Spout where the corn comes out
Man on stack pitching sheaves
Apparatus for sorting types of corn
Man untying sheaves to hand to the feeder
Engine driver
Man untying sheaves to hand to the feeder
Spout at which cobs are delivered

8 Copy and complete the diagram to show how the new system of crop rotation worked.

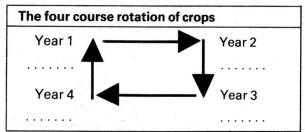

The four course rotation of crops

Year 1	→	Year 2
. . . . . .		. . . . . .
Year 4	←	Year 3
. . . . . .		. . . . . .

Crops: *turnip, wheat, barley, clover.*

9 What were the advantages and disadvantages of both the old and new methods of farming?

3 Transport and machines

Travel in England in the year 1700 was slower and more difficult than it had been fifteen hundred years earlier in Roman times. In the eighteenth century the population was growing, trade was increasing, and new ideas were being worked out in medicine and farming. It was only to be expected that there would be attempts to improve transport, to cope with the increased quantities of goods, and numbers of people who wished to move about the country. The roads were often nothing but muddy tracks in which wagons sometimes sank up to the axles. There were a few coach routes, but travel was slow and uncertain. It often took fourteen days for a coach to go from London to Edinburgh, and coaches left only once a month. Heavy goods were usually carried by river wherever possible, and it was often thought better to go hundreds of kilometres round by river and sea, rather than a few kilometres by land.

Canals

The first main improvement in transport was the construction of canals. A pioneer in this was the Duke of Bridgewater, who wanted a canal to carry coal from his mines to Manchester. He asked a local man, James Brindley, if he could plan such a canal. Brindley had very little education, and could not express himself well, but he seized a large cheese, and quickly carved out a model. The duke was impressed, and told him to carry out his plan. The canal was completed by 1771 and was a success. The price of coal in Manchester was halved. During the next fifty years many canals were constructed, particularly linking the midlands with the four main ports of London, Liverpool, Hull and Bristol, and by 1830 there were over 6000 kilometres of navigable waterways in Britain.

The new industrial age – the Bloomfield Iron Works at Tipton, Staffordshire.

Roads

Increased trade had led to the construction of canals. Then the canals led to an even greater increase in trade. But travel by water was slow, and the question of making good roads was tackled. The first scientific road maker was John Metcalfe. He was blind, but in spite of this he had the land surveyed, and was able to plan routes which avoided steep slopes and boggy land. His roads had solid foundations and a good surface. To avoid the deep ruts and mud on the old roads, vehicles often used to leave the track, and drive across the open country alongside, so the roads were often very wide. The new roads were quite narrow, and where they followed the old ones, they often left wide grass verges. In some roads these can still be seen today.

Many English roads, both old and new, often had sharp right-angle bends, where they followed the old right of way tracks which led along the sides of the large open fields. With the old slow farm carts this did not matter much, but when fast coaches came into use, they proved to be very inconvenient, and where possible the sharp bends were removed, but sometimes an important land-owner would refuse to allow a straight course, to be made across his land, so the roads had to be made with awkward sharp corners. Some of these still remain today, to the annoyance of fast motor traffic.

Other road makers followed Metcalfe, particularly John Macadam. By 1830 thousands of kilometres of good roads were linking the towns of Britain, and thousands of beautifully made coaches were travelling daily averaging twenty kilometres an hour (twelve and half miles an hour) on long journeys of up to 160 kilometres (100 miles). Inns were built at convenient stages along the roads, and horses were changed at lightning speed, while passengers snatched a bite to eat or a drink. Hundreds of thousands of coach horses were reared, and lighter, faster and more comfortable coaches were built. Large wagons for goods were made, and the pack horse became a thing of the past.

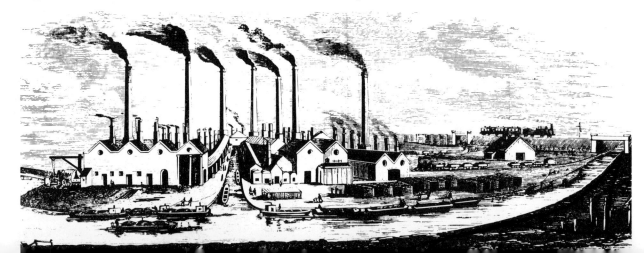

A crowded train on the Stockton to Darlington railway.

Turnpikes

The new well-made roads needed to be kept in good condition, and the repair of many stretches of road was undertaken by certain people in the area, in return for payment of a toll by those using them. These sections of road had toll gates, called turns, across them, where the tolls were collected. They were known as turnpike roads.

Steam

No sooner had the roads been constructed and a prosperous coaching industry developed than another invention began to destroy it again. This was the steam engine. Steam engines of a kind had been used from about AD 1700, to pump water from mines. A great advance in steam engines was made by James Watt in 1769. He altered them so that they were much more efficient, and enabled them to turn the wheeled machines which had been invented to spin yarn and to weave cloth. At first these machines had been worked by water wheels, and the factories or mills had been built beside the rivers, but with the coming of Watt's steam engines, large factories were built in the growing towns of Lancashire and Yorkshire. Yarn and cloth could be made much more quickly and cheaply in these factories, and the people who worked at spinning and weaving in their homes were forced to go to work in the mills. Britain was soon producing vast quantities of cloth and selling it abroad.

Locomotives

Meanwhile a second great advance in the use of steam had occurred: the making of the steam locomotive, so that steam not only turned wheeled machines, but drove the machine itself along.

George Stephenson is often spoken of as the inventor of the steam locomotive, but William Murdock had built a working model of a steam road wagon when Stephenson was only three years old. A number of inventors had constructed locomotives by 1830, but Stephenson's Rocket proved to be the best.

The first public railway with steam locomotives was opened in 1825 between Stockton and Darlington. The first train was driven by Stephenson. It had wagons of coal and flour, and one carriage with passengers. The top speed was about ten miles per hour (sixteen km.), and at that speed the chimney became red hot. For a time the horse-drawn vehicles using the railway seemed so much better than steam trains that the use of steam engines was almost given up. Then better engines were constructed, and steam trains ran regularly.

In 1830 the Liverpool and Manchester railway was opened. Stephenson's Rocket reached a speed of forty-six kilometres an hour. The railway was so successful that within the next twenty years thousands of kilometres of railways were constructed, linking all the chief towns of Britain. Gangs of workmen, known as navvies, many of them Irish, were employed in constructing them. Soon Britain was making railways in Europe and many other parts of the world, often sending gangs of navvies to construct them, and exporting huge quantities of rails, coaches and engines.

The changes in industry at this time came to be known as the Industrial Revolution.

One of the hazards of road travel – driver and passengers struggle to free the Royal Mail coach stuck in a snow drift. An engraving of 1825.

Transport and machines

Exercises and things to do

London to Exeter

1814
22 hours

1903
3½ hours

1983
2½ hours

1 Write out, filling in the blanks. One – stands for each missing letter.

Until the eighteenth century goods were usually carried by ––––– or by ––– wherever possible. The first great improvement was the making of ––––––. Soon these were connecting the midlands with the main –––––. Trade increased, but travel by water was ––––, and it became clear that good ––––– must be made. The most famous roadmaker in Britain was –––– –––––––. Some parts of well-made roads were called –––––––––, and people using them paid a ––––, which was used to keep them in good repair. The next great advance in travel was the invention of the –––––––––, driven by –––––. In 1825 the first public ––––––– was opened between –––––––– and –––––––––––. Within a few years there were thousands of kilometres of –––––––.

2 The heads and tails of these statements have been mixed. Write them out correctly.

(a) James Brindley	(1) was the first scientific road maker.
(b) Steam engines	(2) linked the midlands with the main ports.
(c) John Metcalfe	(3) drove the first railway train.
(d) Canals	(4) were a means of collecting tolls.
(e) James Stephenson	(5) made canals.
(f) Turnpikes	(6) were first used to pump water from the mines.

3 *Statements of fact* Write out the four statements in each group in what you think is their order of importance or interest. Say in each group why you decided to put one particular statement first.

(a) Travel in Britain
  (1) was slow and uncomfortable in 1700.
  (2) was greatly improved on roads made by Metcalfe and Macadam.
  (3) was often on turnpikes for which users had to pay tolls.
  (4) by 1830 was using fast coaches which linked the main towns.

(b) Canals in Britain
  (1) were cut mainly between 1771 and 1830.
  (2) connected the midlands with the four main ports.
  (3) began with the Duke of Bridgewater's canal to take coal to Manchester.
  (4) led to a great increase in trade.

(c) Steam engines
  (1) were first used to pump water from mines.
  (2) were improved by James Watt.
  (3) led to factory production and railway travel.
  (4) were adapted to locomotives by Murdock, Stephenson and others.

4 *The right order* Write these out in the order in which they happened.

(a) Brindley's first canal
(b) Stockton and Darlington railway was opened.
(c) Steam engines were used for pumping water.
(d) The coaching industry was almost ruined.

5 *The main idea* Write out the one sentence which tells what you think is the main idea of this topic.

(a) Growing population and trade led to great developments in transport.
(b) Brindley began the cutting of a great system of canals.
(c) By 1830 a network of good roads had been constructed.
(d) After 1830 railway transport began to take the place of road transport.

6 Write a story about the mail coach in the snow drift. Use all the details on the engraving to help you.

A steam-driven printing press used by 'The Times' newspaper company in the early nineteenth century. Steam engines were used in many industries to replace traditional forms of power.

7 Study the picture of the Stockton–Darlington Railway and answer the following questions:

(a) How many wagons can you see?
(b) How many coaches can you see?
(c) Why is the railway coach similar to the Royal Mail coach?
(d) Why do some people travel in coaches and others in wagons?
(e) Why do men stand between the wagons?
(f) What else would be needed apart from coal to drive the locomotive? Where was this stored?

8 Draw the front cover of a booklet advertising Bloomfield Iron Works. Stress the product, the modern methods used, and the availability of different forms of transport.

9 Study the map and complete the grid.

Start	Canal/River	Destination
London		Liverpool
Birmingham		Liverpool
Liverpool		Hull
Hull		Bristol

10 Using library books write a paragraph on each of the following: George Stephenson, Isambard Kingdom Brunel, the railway navvies.

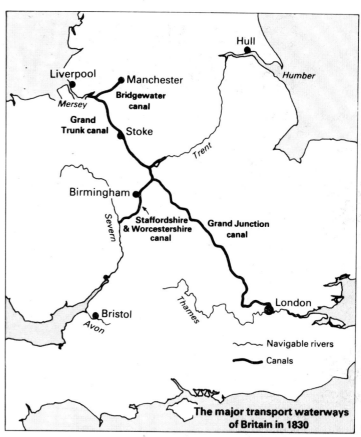

The cross-shaped canal network which connected northern and midland industrial areas to the major ports.

Photographer S. Newton recorded the building of the Great Central Railway Company's line from Nottingham to London (1894–99). Men and horses work alongside a new excavator.

4 The French Revolution: Napoleon

A doctor becomes a revolutionary

Jean Paul Marat was a successful doctor in Paris. He travelled to Britain, studying science, and was honoured with the degree of M D at the university of St Andrews. He returned to Paris and gained many wealthy patients; but he also saw how the ordinary people in France lived. He saw the hovels of the poverty-stricken peasants, and the beggars and slums of Paris. Their miserable life horrified him. He gave up his wealthy patients and their world of luxury; he left the magnificent houses of the nobles. He left his study of medicine and science. He felt that the way in which the country was run was wrong. He worked for revolution.

Revolution begins

Other people were thinking the same. In 1789 the country was so unsettled that King Louis XVI decided to call the States General, the French Parliament. It had not met for 175 years, and there was great excitement. Thousands of hungry men and women swarmed into Paris, rioting and demanding bread. The soldiers hesitated to fire upon the crowds. A new government of the city was formed, and an army of citizens was set up, called the National Guard. The soldiers helped, and the great fortress and prison of the Bastille was singled out for the initial attack, which began the revolution.

The governor surrenders the Bastille to the revolutionaries on 14 July 1789.

The Rights of Man

A National Assembly was formed, and it drew up a Declaration of the Rights of Man. All people were to be free to speak and write as they wished, all were to be treated equally before the law. Liberty, Equality and Fraternity (brotherhood) was the slogan. All titles except that of King were abolished. A nobleman named Mirabeau led the Assembly, and the king agreed to everything.

But this was not enough for Marat. He saw that the poor were as hungry as ever, while the king and the officers still lived in luxury. Marat wrote articles demanding the death of Mirabeau, of the king, of the officers, and of the nobles. The leaders of the Assembly ordered his arrest. Marat fled. He hid in cellars and attics, still writing, pouring scorn on the timid leaders of the revolution.

New leaders

In 1792 things changed. Most of the nobles had fled, and had persuaded the Austrians and Prussians to invade France, to restore them and the king to power. The French people fought for the freedom which the revolution had brought them. They turned savagely on their enemies and drove them back. The king tried to escape, but he was caught and brought back. Mirabeau died, and Danton and Robespierre took his place. Marat came out of hiding, and joined them in the government. Now he had his way: the king and queen were executed. 'The kings of Europe would challenge us,' said Danton. 'We throw them the head of a king.'

The nobles who had not managed to escape were executed, but for Marat this was not enough. He wanted to see all wealth shared equally among all the people. 'Who can say he has a right to eat, so long as anyone is without bread?' he said. He scarcely slept. Day and night he sat scribbling articles calling for more and more executions. He broke down under the strain, but still he sat, writing, writing, writing, accusing everyone, for to his clouded mind, the world seemed full of traitors to the revolution. Then he was stabbed to death by Charlotte Corday, whose friends he had denounced. 'I have killed a monster,' she said, 'to save hundreds of thousands.'

Danton came to think that too many people were being put to death, but Robespierre turned upon Danton and had him beheaded. 'Show my head to the people,' cried Danton, 'they don't see such a head everyday.'

War

France was at war with Austria, Prussia, Holland, Sweden and Britain. The government put the defence of the country in the hands of a young army officer named Napoleon Bonaparte. In France the revolution was over, but not the war, nor the ideas of the revolution. French soldiers carried these to other countries in Europe. They offered to help their people to gain their freedom from kings and nobles. The people were told that they were no longer serfs, and they were encouraged to elect an Assembly.

Napoleon, first consul and emperor of the French

A new French government made Napoleon first consul, and then emperor. He set up a fairer system of taxes, started many schools, and had a code of fair laws drawn up. He believed that everyone who had talent should have a chance to rise in the world. 'Every soldier,' he said, 'carries a field marshal's baton in his knapsack.'

The war continued. Napoleon had conquered most of the countries of western Europe, but Britain defied him. He decided to invade Britain. His army was drawn up on the coast, and 1500 boats waited to take it across the Channel, 'that ditch' as he called it, but they never sailed. The British navy commanded the sea, and prevented him from carrying out his threat to 'destroy this nation of shopkeepers'. He tried to ruin Britain's trade by commanding all the ports of Europe to be closed against British ships. Britain replied by stopping almost all Europe's sea-borne trade. This led to a quarrel between Napoleon and Alexander I of Russia. In 1812 Napoleon raised a great new army and advanced into Russia. The Russians retreated, destroying everything which might be helpful to the French invaders.

The French entered Moscow. The city was deserted, and Alexander made no offer to give in and make peace. Napoleon waited. He grew anxious: winter was coming on. Fires broke out in many parts of the city. He decided to retreat, and slowly the Grand Army turned back over the desolated countryside. Winter closed in. Through icy blizzards the French stumbled on. Many died from cold and starvation; many were killed by the Russians. Almost the whole French army was wiped out.

The power of Napoleon as shown by the French painter, David.

This Leeds ware chamber pot of 1810 shows that the English, unlike the French, were not respectful of Napoleon.

Napoleon left the remnants of his army and returned to France, to raise more troops, but the struggle was coming to an end. Countries he had conquered began to rise against him. In 1815 Napoleon was defeated by British, Belgians and Prussians at Waterloo. He surrendered, and was sent to the little island of St Helena, in the far Atlantic, where he died in 1821.

Exercises and things to do

1 Write out, filling in the blanks. One – stands for each missing letter.

There was much poverty and discontent in France in the year ————. King ————— the XVI called the —————— General, the French ——————————, which had not met for ——— years. There were riots, and the citizens formed an army called the ———————— —————, and set up a National ————————, which drew up a Declaration of the —————— of ———. Their motto was ———————, ———————— and Fraternity.

The nobles fled from France, and the ———— tried to escape. He was caught and ————————. Danton, ——————————— and ————— became the leaders. Austria declared ——— on France, followed by Prussia, ———————, ——————— and ——————. The French had a great leader in ——————————, who conquered much of western —————— for a time.

2 The heads and tails of these statements have been mixed. Write them out correctly.

(a) Marat   (1) was brought to execution by Robespierre.

(b) Napoleon   (2) became leader of the Revolution in 1792.

(c) Alexander   (3) was first leader of the Assembly.

(d) Danton   (4) gave up everything to work for the revolution.

(e) Mirabeau   (5) was ruler of Russia.

(f) Robespierre   (6) led the French army to many victories.

(g) Liberty   (7) means treating all like brothers.

(h) Equality   (8) means making all men and women free.

(i) Fraternity   (9) means giving all people fair shares.

(j) The States General   (10) was the army of citizens.

(k) The Assembly   (11) was the old Parliament of France.

(l) The National Guard   (12) was the first revolutionary government.

A cartoon of the Duke of Wellington who led the British army at Waterloo and gave his name to the wellington boot.

3 *Statements of fact* Write out the four statements in each group, in what you think is their order of importance or interest. Say in each group why you decided to put that particular statement first.

(a) The French Revolution
  (1) began in 1789.
  (2) was an attempt to change the way France was governed.
  (3) abolished all titles.
  (4) drew up the Declaration of the Rights of Man.

(b) The French revolutionaries
  (1) executed their king and queen.
  (2) executed one another.
  (3) threw back the Austrian invaders.
  (4) put Napoleon in charge of the country's defence.

(c) Napoleon
  (1) made taxes more fair.
  (2) drew up a new code of laws.
  (3) improved education, law and taxes.
  (4) invaded Russia, but was forced to retreat.

4 *The right order* Write these out in the order in which they happened.

(a) Napoleon was chosen to lead the defence of France.
(b) The king called the States General.
(c) The retreat from Moscow.
(d) Mirabeau led the Assembly.

5 *The main idea* Write out the one sentence which tells what you think is the main idea of this topic.

(a) Marat gave up being a doctor to work for revolution.
(b) The king called the first Parliament for 175 years.
(c) After great successes, Napoleon was finally defeated.
(d) The French Revolution spread ideas of freedom for the ordinary people to other parts of Europe.

6 Using the information in questions 1, 2 and 3 (a) and (b) on this page, complete the front page of a newspaper bringing news of the French Revolution.

7 Study the map and make a list of countries which came under Napoleon's control.

8 Read page 17 again and explain why Napoleon did not invade England.

9 Explain why the rich people and rulers of countries outside France would fear the spread of revolutionary ideas.

10 Study the cartoon and complete these exercises:

(a) List the towns shown.
(b) How is the French army shown?
(c) What is 'General Frost' saying to 'Boney'?
(d) What do you think was the main cause of Napoleon's defeat?

11 *Research projects*
Prepare short illustrated projects on:

(a) The life of Napoleon Bonaparte
(b) Nelson and the Battle of Trafalgar
(c) Wellington and the Battle of Waterloo

An English cartoon of 1812 showing Napoleon and his army retreating from Moscow during the harsh Russian winter. The title was 'General Frost Shaving Little Boney'.

5 Revolutions in Europe

There are many nations in Europe. Today most of them have a country and a government of their own, but in the early nineteenth century some of them were ruled by others. The Austrians ruled over the Hungarians, Czechs, Slovaks and many Italians. The Ottoman or Turkish Empire contained the Greeks, Bulgarians, Serbians and others. Holland ruled the Belgians, and the Swedes ruled the Norwegians. Most of the Poles were ruled by Russia, some by Austria and some by Prussia. The German people were divided into thirty-nine different states. Many Germans thought that there ought to be one country of Germany for all Germans. The French Revolution had spread ideas of freedom, and these European nations wanted to be free to rule themselves. This was known as nationalism.

The Congress of Vienna

After the defeat of Napoleon, the kings and foreign ministers of the chief European countries met at the Congress of Vienna to settle the problems created by the war. Czar Alexander spoke for Russia, Prince Metternich for Austria, King Frederick William for Prussia, Talleyrand for France and Lord Castlereagh for Britain. They could have worked for freedom and justice for all peoples, but their main aims were to maintain their own power, and to prevent any more revolutions. Lord Castlereagh did not agree with interfering in other countries, so Britain did not join the Holy Alliance, as it was called, but it did join the others in the Concert of Europe, to unite to keep the Bonaparte family out of France, and to discuss ways of keeping peace in Europe. The French royal family who had been driven from the throne in France in the revolution was restored to the throne, and Charles X was made king.

The Congress of Vienna forced the Protestant Dutch to give up their republic, and join the French-speaking Catholic Belgians in the kingdom of the Netherlands. Norway was handed over to the king of Sweden. Venice and much of northern Italy was given to Austria. Most of Catholic Poland was given to Orthodox Christian Russia, most of the rest of it to Protestant Prussia, and some to Austria. French-speaking Savoy was combined with part of Italy to form the Kingdom of Sardinia. The thirty-nine independent states of Germany were formed, with a part of Prussia and a part of Austria, into the German Confederation. It is not surprising that peace did not last for very long.

A year of revolution

The subject peoples planned, plotted and fought for their independence, and during the next 100 years most of them succeeded. In France, when King Charles X began to rule without Parliament, and to take away the right to vote from millions of Frenchmen, the bells of Paris again called the people to arms. Once more barricades were raised in the streets, and Paris rose against the king, to fight for liberty, equality and the rights of the people. In 1830 Charles fled. This second revolution did not bring a republic, but another king, Louis Philippe. It was hoped that he would be a different kind of king. He walked about the city, smiling and shaking hands with the people. He carried, not a sword, but an umbrella.

Belgium and Poland

The idea of revolution spread: the Belgians rose against the Dutch. Britain and France supported them, and the kingdom of Belgium was set up. Also in 1830 the Poles rose against the Russians. No-one supported them, and they were crushed. Not until after the First World War in 1918 did the Poles get a government of their own.

Britain

In England there was unrest in 1830, when farm workers revolted, to try to get better wages, which were extremely low. They burned ricks and destroyed the threshing machines which spoiled their chances of earning a little extra. The troops were called out, and the revolt collapsed. Nine of the ringleaders were hanged, and nearly five hundred transported as convicts. The farm workers had made their final effort, their last hopes were gone, and they relapsed into despair.

Others in Britain who were still unable to vote and were very disappointed at the way in which the country was governed demanded that Parliament should be reformed, and more people be given the right to vote for members of parliament. There were riots in various places, and in 1832 a Reform Bill was passed, which gave the vote

A contemporary cartoon showing Louis Philippe becoming increasingly unpopular.

The top map shows how Europe was divided up after the Congress of Vienna. The bottom map shows how Europe altered after the revolts in this chapter and the changes mentioned in chapter 9 (pp. 36–37).

mostly to middle class men such as male land-owners and university graduates. The mass of working men and all women had to wait for their rights to be granted.

Italy

Meanwhile in Italy a leader of those who longed for freedom from Austrian rule had begun to fill young people with enthusiasm. His name was Mazzini. He founded Young Italy, a society which began to work for freedom. He hoped for a united republic of all Italy. He even dreamed of a world republic.

Another year of revolution

In 1848 the people throughout Italy revolted against their Austrian rulers. The Czechs, the Hungarians, the Serbs and the Croats also rose against the Austrians. The Czar of Russia sent an army to help the Austrian government, and all the revolts were beaten; but the struggle continued, and the people waited for their opportunity. Mazzini's writings were forbidden in Italy, but they were smuggled into the country hidden in bricks by an English brickmaker.

By 1848 the French had grown dissatisfied with Louis Philippe, and there was a third French Revolution. Louis Philippe offered to give up the throne to his grandson, but the Paris crowds shouted, 'Down with all kings' and a republic was proclaimed. The republicans could not agree. Barricades were thrown up in the streets, and there was fierce fighting. Thousands were killed. Then Louis Napoleon, nephew of Napoleon Bonaparte was elected as president. Soon he persuaded the people of France to make him emperor, with the title of Napoleon III.

Besides the revolts throughout the Austrian Empire, there were risings in many German states, where the people demanded parliaments. Most of the rulers promised what they were asked, but soon the parliaments lost what little power they had been given. In Austria too in 1848 the Austrian people themselves revolted against their government and demanded a parliament, but the army crushed them. In England there was talk of revolution. Vast crowds demanded the vote for all men, but the crowds dispersed, and nothing came of their demands for a long time. The fight for national freedom, and the struggle for democracy were not to be won easily.

Exercises and things to do

1 Write out, filling in the blanks. One – stands for each missing letter.

After the defeat of France in 1815, the chief – – – – – – – – leaders met at the – – – – – – – – of – – – – – – to settle many problems. Their main aim was to prevent any more – – – – – – – – – –, but as they put several – – – – – – – under foreign rulers, some of them soon began to start – – – – – – – – for their – – – – – – – – – – – –. In the year – – – – the French drove out their – – – – and chose – – – – – – – – – – – – to rule them. The Belgians rose against the – – – – –, and the Poles against the – – – – – – – –. In England in 1830 the farm workers revolted against their masters because – – – – – were so – – –, and in 1832 there were riots, demanding that more people should have the – – – – – to – – – – for members of – – – – – – – – – –.

In 1848 there were revolts in – – – – – –, – – – – – – –, – – – – – – – and – – – – –.

2 The heads and tails of these statements have been mixed. Write them out correctly.

After 1815

(a) Germany   (1) ruled over Hungarians, Czechs and Italians.
(b) France   (2) ruled over Poland.
(c) Sweden   (3) had riots calling for better wages.
(d) Austria   (4) was divided into thirty-nine states.
(e) Metternich   (5) called upon the Italians to revolt.
(f) Russia   (6) ruled over Belgium.
(g) Holland   (7) was soon tired of King Charles.
(h) England   (8) ruled over Norway.
(i) Mazzini   (9) spoke for Austria at the Congress of Vienna.

3 *Statements of fact* Write out the four statements in each group in what you think is their order of importance or interest. Say in each group why you decided to put one particular statement first.

(a) In the early nineteenth century
    (1) the Austrians ruled over Poles, Hungarians and Italians.
    (2) Holland ruled over the Belgians.
    (3) the Norwegians were ruled by the Swedes.
    (4) many European nations were under foreign rule.

(b) Nationalism
    (1) is the desire of nations to rule themselves.
    (2) was encouraged by the French Revolution.
    (3) was often opposed by kings.
    (4) led to many revolts by nations who wanted independence.

(c) In the year 1848
    (1) there were widespread revolts against the Austrians.
    (2) the third French Revolution took place.
    (3) there were revolutions in France, Austria, Italy and Germany.

4 *The right order* Write these out in the order in which they happened.

(a) Louis Napoleon became emperor of France.
(b) The Reform Bill was passed in Britain.
(c) Louis Philippe gave up the throne.
(d) Belgium gained independence.

5 *The main idea* Write out the one sentence which tells what you think is the main idea of this topic.
(a) The French had three revolutions.
(b) The Belgians gained their independence.
(c) After the French Revolution many European nations began to struggle for freedom.
(d) 1848 was the Year of Revolutions.

Poor labourers tried to protect their jobs by smashing the new machines. Their anger had little effect.

Napoleon's victors met at the Congress of Vienna in 1815. After many years of war they wanted peace, stability, and an end to French revolutionary ideas and military aggression. Here the leaders of Britain (Duke of Wellington; labelled 4), Russia (Czar Alexander I: 2), Austria (Francis I: 1), Prussia (Frederic William III: 3) and other nations consider plans for peace.

6 Which men represented the following countries at the Congress of Vienna: Austria, Prussia, Russia and Britain?

7 Write a paragraph explaining the aims and results of the Congress of Vienna.

8 Write a newspaper report on either (a) the French uprising of 1830 or (b) the English riots of 1830. Use your imagination to fill in the details.

9 Write a letter to your local newspaper explaining your actions.

10 What was the Reform Bill of 1832 and why was it important?

11 What were the reasons for the revolts (a) against the Austrians, (b) against Louis Philippe and (c) against the German rulers?

12 Read 'Another year of revolution' on page 21 and complete this chart:

Revolts in 1848	
People who revolted	Revolt directed against . . .
Italians Czechs	*Austrian rulers*

Revolutions spread across Europe during 1848. In Vienna students erected barricades, as shown here. They demanded a parliament.

6 Explorers and missionaries in Africa

Until the end of the eighteenth century little was known of Africa, apart from the coastal districts where there were European trading posts. By far the most important trade was that in slaves.

The slave trade

The Arabs obtained slaves mainly from the east coastal regions and the Sudan, while raiding parties penetrated far inland. They used them largely as house servants, guards of the women and their palaces, and as fighting men in their navies. The Europeans obtained theirs mainly from the west and south coasts, where the coastal tribes sent large slave raiding expeditions far into the interior, driving their victims by the lash, roped together in long trains, back to the coast where they were sold to the white traders. The slaves were then crowded on to slave ships and taken to the colonies in America, where they laboured in the plantations under burning suns.

Very few Europeans had been interested in trying to penetrate into the interior of Africa, and it remained 'The Unknown Continent', or 'Darkest Africa', a land of burning deserts, disease ridden swamps and forests and hostile people. Portuguese missionaries had made a few attempts to carry Christianity to the African people in the seventeenth century, but they were driven out.

Exploration

Towards the end of the eighteenth century there was a change, and several explorers became interested in finding the true courses of the rivers Nile and Niger. James Bruce voyaged up the Nile, then crossed the desert to Gondar on the Red Sea. From there he penetrated to the source of a river, but it was not that of the main stream of the Nile.

A group of slaves, chained and collared together, being driven to the coast by armed native guards.

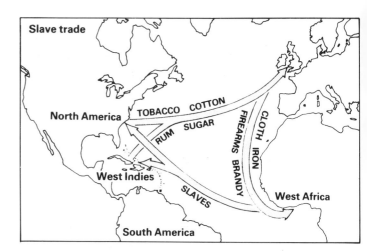

The Niger

In 1788 Sir Joseph Banks formed the Africa Association, with the object of solving the riddle of the Niger. In 1795 Mungo Park started from the Gambia river, reached the Niger and travelled along it to within 300 kilometres of Timbuktu, but then, 'worn down,' as he said, 'by sickness, exhausted by hunger and fatigue, and half naked' he decided to turn back, as he had nothing left with which to buy food.

In 1805 he tried again. He started with thirty-eight soldiers and seamen. Fever broke out, and only seven reached the Niger alive. They travelled nearly 2000 kilometres down the river. 'I shall sail on,' he wrote, 'or perish in the attempt,' but then hostile natives attacked his little boat, and he was drowned.

Ending the slave trade

At the beginning of the nineteenth century a great change was coming over the attitude of Europeans and Americans to the slave trade. In 1787, William Wilberforce had formed an association in Britain to work for the ending of slavery. In 1792 Denmark ended the slave trade in Danish pos-

sessions. In 1807 the USA stopped the importation of slaves, and British citizens were forbidden to take part in the slave trade, and soon after this most European countries ended the trade in human beings. Instead, hundreds of Christian missionaries went to many parts of Africa, to convert the people to Christianity. They explored the unknown rivers, forests and deserts, learned the native languages, and sometimes worked as doctors and teachers.

None of the early colonies and trading stations had extended very far inland, but in the nineteenth century traders began to follow the missionaries and explorers. There was a growing interest in the great unknown continent, and fresh explorers tried to solve the questions which had puzzled Europeans for centuries: where was the source of the Nile? Did the Niger flow into the Nile, or did it flow to the west, or did it lose itself in the desert sands? Was there really a great city of Timbuktu in the heart of west Africa? Would further opportunities for trade be opened up?

Halfway through the nineteenth century little more was known about the source of the Nile than had been known by the ancient Romans, but in 1856 Speke discovered the great Lake Victoria, from which the Nile flowed.

David Livingstone

The greatest explorer, and the greatest missionary, was David Livingstone. He went to South Africa as a missionary in 1840. With his wife and family he travelled far into the heart of the country by ox-wagon, and then worked among the people for some years as a doctor, teacher and preacher. Then he pushed further north into regions never before visited by Europeans.

He was sickened by the horrors of the slave trade, which was still carried on by the Arabs. He was convinced that the way to end the slave trade was to open up the country to ordinary trade, so that the brutality of the slave trade would become known, and so that the African people could learn to grow crops and produce things which would be more valuable than the slave trade could be. 'I will open up a path into the interior or perish,' he said.

He sent his wife and children back to Britain, and then, starting from Linyanti, he forced a way through forest and swamp, by canoe, on oxen, and on foot, in spite of fever and weakness from lack of food. At last, weak and exhausted by months of walking, he reached the coast at Loanda. There a British naval ship offered to take him home to Britain, but he refused: he had promised to take

Explorer H. M. Stanley looks on as his native helpers carry canoes around the Inkisi Falls.

his native servants back to their homes. He turned, and made the long two year journey back, this time right to the east coast. After sixteen years in Africa he returned to Britain, but he was soon back again, exploring and bringing Christianity, medical knowledge and help to the Africans.

Unfortunately, the traders who followed him often brought alcoholic drink and firearms, which led to misery and destruction. Then came the empire builders, and soon almost all Africa passed under European control.

Slavery

Over two million negroes were transported to the English American colonies, and nearly three quarters of a million to Jamaica in less than a century. Over 70,000 slaves were taken to America every year towards the end of the eighteenth century.

Britain abolished slavery throughout the British Empire in 1833. £20 million were paid to the slave owners in the West Indies as compensation, and £1¼ million to those in South Africa.

Exercises and things to do

1 Write out, filling in the blanks. One – stands for each missing letter.

For a very long time Africa was called the
———— ————. Late in the
————— century, exploration of the rivers
———— and ————— began. At the same time people in Europe and America began to try and end the
————— —————.

By the year 1856 the true courses of the Niger and Nile had been discovered, and
————————— had penetrated far into
——————— parts of Africa, teaching the people about ————————— and acting as
———————— and ————————.

2 The heads and tails of these statements have been mixed. Write them out correctly.

(a) The Arabs	(1) obtained their slaves from west Africa.
(b) James Bruce	(2) explored much of the river Niger.
(c) Denmark	(3) stopped importing slaves in 1807.
(d) Wilberforce	(4) went as a missionary to Africa in 1840.
(e) Mungo Park	(5) looked for the source of the Nile.
(f) The USA	(6) ended her part in the slave trade in 1792.
(g) Livingstone	(7) formed an association to stop the slave trade.
(h) The Europeans	(8) used slaves mainly from east Africa in their navies.

3 *Statements of fact* Write out the four statements in each group, in what you think is their order of importance or interest. Say in each group why you decided to put one particular statement first.

(a) European knowledge of Africa
  (1) was little greater in 1780 than it was in Roman times.
  (2) was limited to coastal regions until the nineteenth century.
  (3) was extended by explorers after about 1780.
  (4) grew as explorers tried to trace the courses of the main African rivers.

(b) David Livingstone
  (1) was a great explorer.
  (2) hated the slave trade.
  (3) explored Africa to help the Africans and to end the slave trade.
  (4) crossed Africa from east to west.

(c) The slave trade
  (1) was carried on by Arabs and Europeans.
  (2) was ended by most Europeans in the early nineteenth century.
  (3) supplied labour for the American plantations.
  (4) brought division and enmity between African tribes.

4 *The right order* Write these out in the order in which they happened.

(a) Livingstone crossed Africa from east to west.
(b) Speke discovered Lake Victoria.
(c) Most Europeans abolished the slave trade.

5 *The main idea* Write out the one sentence which tells what you think is the main idea of this topic.

(a) European explorers opened up the interior of Africa to trade and to European ideas in the nineteenth century.
(b) Knowledge of Africa grew very slowly.
(c) Many men died trying to explore Africa.
(d) Livingstone was the greatest explorer and missionary to Africa.

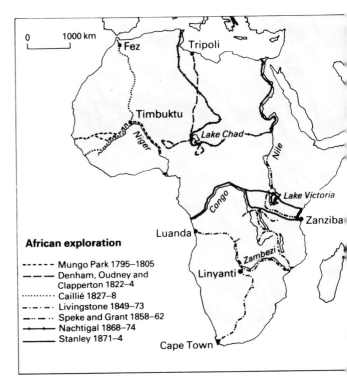

African exploration

- - - - - Mungo Park 1795–1805
— — — Denham, Oudney and Clapperton 1822–4
. . . . Caillié 1827–8
— . — . — Livingstone 1849–73
— .. — .. Speke and Grant 1858–62
—+—+— Nachtigal 1868–74
————— Stanley 1871–4

An African carving of Queen Victoria.

6 Copy the map on page 24.

7 Why were slaves taken from Africa to (a) the West Indies and (b) the United States?

8 Copy the carving of Queen Victoria.

9 The exploration of Africa caught the imagination of Europeans during the nineteenth century. Which form of exploration has been of great interest during this century?

10 Draw the time line below and complete it by using information from pages 24 and 25.

Slavery				
1700	**1787**	**1792**	**1807**	**1833**
Arabs, Europeans obtain slaves from Africa				slavery abolished in British Empire

11 What do you think would be the reaction of those Africans who came into contact with:

(a) slavers   (c) missionaries
(b) explorers   (d) traders?

12 Using other books write a short biography of either Mungo Park, William Wilberforce or David Livingstone.

13 *Project*
Below are the titles of illustrations from Stanley's book *In Darkest Africa*:

'A typical village on the Arowimi'
'Attacking an elephant on the Ituri river'
'Diagram of our forest camp'
'The fight with the Arisibba cannibals'
'Bridge across the Ituri river'
'One of Mazamboni's Warriors'

Using these, the map on page 26, the information on page 25, and material from other books write an illustrated account of one of Stanley's journeys in Africa.

Europeans thought it a duty to bring Christianity to Africa. They faced disease, hostility and isolation. Despite the conditions, these women missionaries wore European dress.

Technology, like Christianity, was also taken to Africa by Europeans. In this nineteenth century advert, electricity is shown transforming the 'Dark Continent'.

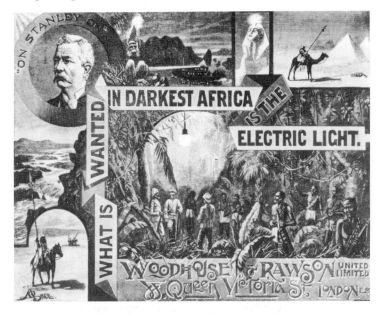

14 Measure the distance on the map that Livingstone travelled from the southern tip of Africa to Luanda and back to the east coast. Using the scale, work out roughly how many kilometres he travelled.

7 China and Japan in the nineteenth century

A vast empire

In the year 1800 the emperor of China ruled over a vast empire, and in addition, the rulers of Korea, Annam, Nepal and Burma regarded the emperor of China as their overlord, and paid him tribute. The empire was governed by a great civil service of people who had passed examinations which were open to almost everybody except actors and soldiers.

Most of the people were peasants, living in villages and small towns, but there were some cities as large and splendid as any in the world at the time. The population of China was probably about 300 million, greater than that of all the European countries put together.

The Chinese worshipped their ancestors, and honoured their great teacher Confucius. After 1601 Christian missionaries were allowed in China, and by 1700 there were about 250,000 Chinese Christians, but after that the number decreased.

Foreign devils

As the Europeans became increasingly fond of Chinese tea, silk and porcelain, an important trade grew up between China and Europe, but non-Chinese merchants had to use the port of Canton; all others were closed to them. The Chinese despised all traders, and considered all foreigners to be barbarians or 'foreign devils'. They would not allow foreigners to have Chinese servants, and no Chinese might teach his language to a foreigner. Communication was carried on in Pidgin English, a mixture of English, Portuguese and Indian words. (Pidgin was the way the Chinese pronounced the word business, so Pidgin English was business English.) Foreigners were not allowed out of their quarters, and could not go into the city or surrounding countryside.

One of the chief articles of trade was opium, a very strong drug which was grown in India and exported to China. The Chinese emperor forbade

Japan, a country cut off from the world

After the first friendly European contact with Japan in the sixteenth century, the Japanese stopped almost all trade with other nations. In 1636 all Japanese were forbidden to leave the country, and Japanese then abroad were forbidden to return to Japan. All foreigners were driven from the country except a few Dutch traders who were allowed to remain, provided that they stayed on one little islet, and prostrated themselves before the Shogun, who ruled the country on behalf of the emperor. Only one Dutch trading ship was allowed to visit Japan each year. The great fleet of Japanese merchant ships that had been built was left to rot away.

For the next 220 years the Japanese remained cut off from almost the whole of the rest of the world. They knew nothing of the invention of the steam engine and other things which were transforming the life of the people of the west. When the great empty spaces of Canada, Australia and Siberia were being included in European empires, the Japanese remained shut up in their small island home. Later, when they wanted new lands for their rapidly increasing population, it was too late, there were very few undeveloped lands available.

America opens the door

In 1853 Commodore Perry of the United States navy arrived off the Japanese coast with a letter from the American president, asking the Japanese to open up trade. The American steamships, the telegraph and a model railway greatly interested the Japanese. The big guns impressed them. They agreed to allow the foreigners to trade, and to live under their own laws, and not those of Japan.

Making a modern Japan

In 1867 the emperor took over the government from the Shogun, and began the greatest series of changes any country had ever embarked upon. The Japanese decided to bring their country up to date by copying the Europeans and Americans. They started education for all, in schools modelled on those of the United States. All men had to serve in the army, which was trained in German methods by German officers, or the navy, built with the help of the British. Railways and factories were built, and Japanese trade increased rapidly.

its import, but both British and Chinese merchants smuggled a great deal of opium into the country. There were many disputes. In June, 1839 the Chinese governor of Canton threw thousands of chests of the 'foreign mud' as he called the opium, into the sea.

The Opium War

In July 1840 a Chinese sailor was killed in a fight with drunken English sailors. When the man who had struck the blow could not be found, Captain Elliot, in charge of the British settlement, refused to send someone else instead, as Chinese law demanded, and the British merchants moved to Hong Kong to get away from the trouble. Shots were fired, and the first Anglo-Chinese war, sometimes called the Opium War, broke out. The Chinese were no match for the well-armed British ships and troops, and were soon forced to give in. The Chinese agreed to pay several million pounds, to open several ports to British traders, and to hand over Hong Kong to Britain for her to use for the next 150 years. Other treaties were soon made, giving America and some European countries trading rights in China, and the chance to build railways there. Foreign residents in China were

Distrust of French Catholic missionaries led to the massacre of priests at De Tien-Tsin in 1870.

given the right to be judged by the laws of their own country, and not by Chinese law. The Chinese resented the interference in Chinese affairs by Europeans. In 1900 there was a rebellion against the 'foreign devils', but the Chinese were hopelessly outfought. It was to be quite some time before China could regain her complete independence.

A kind of parliament was set up, but the emperor and his ministers retained most of the power. They wanted to build up an empire, in the European fashion. They forced war upon China in 1894, and Japan gained control of Korea and Formosa. Port Arthur was also taken, but Russia, Germany and France then forced Japan to give it back to China. Three years later, France, Germany and Britain took some Chinese ports for themselves, and Russia seized Port Arthur. The Japanese were furious, and waited for a chance for revenge. It came early in the next century.

Japan, a great power

Meanwhile the great powers began to treat Japan as one of themselves, and Japanese troops joined with British, French and Germans to march on Peking, capital of China, to put down the nationalist Boxer rising of the Chinese against all foreigners. By this time all foreign powers had agreed to give up the right of their people in Japan to live under their own laws, and all became subject to Japanese law.

A nineteenth century Japanese view of European influence. Note the women's dresses.

Exercises and things to do

1 Write out, filling in the blanks. One – stands for each missing letter.

A Chinese depiction of a 'foreign devil' – probably an English sailor who was smoking.

In the year 1800 China was a – – – – – – – – – – –, with some splendid – – – – – – and thousands of – – – – – – – –. For a long time the Chinese had a very poor opinion of – – – – – – and – – – – – – – – – –, and closed all ports except – – – – – – to foreign – – – – – – – – –. In 1839 a quarrel about trade in – – – – – led to a war between – – – – – – – and – – – – –, and the – – – – – – – were forced to open other – – – – – to – – – – – – – and other – – – – – – – – traders.

For a long time the Japanese cut themselves off from the rest of the – – – – –, but in the year – – – – the United States persuaded them to open up – – – – –, and to allow – – – – – – – – – to live in Japan. Soon the Japanese decided to copy – – – – – – – – education, German – – – – methods and the – – – – – – – – – – – –, and so made Japan a – – – – – – – – – –.

2 The heads and tails of these statements have been mixed. Write them out correctly.

(a) Confucius   (1) ruled Japan.
(b) The Shogun   (2) was a Chinese teacher.
(c) Canton   (3) was handed over to Britain.
(d) In 1900   (4) the Japanese decided to modernize their country.
(e) Hong Kong   (5) was the first Chinese port opened to foreigners.
(f) In 1867   (6) the Chinese rebelled against the foreigners.

3 *Statements of fact* Write out the four statements in each group in what you think is their order of importance or interest. Say in each group why you decided to put one particular statement first.

(a) In the early nineteenth century
 (1) China was the most populous country in the world.
 (2) the Chinese lived mainly in villages.
 (3) the Chinese were governed by civil servants who had passed an examination.
 (4) the Chinese were ruled by an emperor.

(b) The Japanese for a long time
 (1) feared that contact with other countries would be bad for the country.
 (2) stopped almost all trade with Europe.
 (3) forbade all Japanese to leave the country.
 (4) broke almost all contact with the rest of the world.

(c) In the late nineteenth century the Japanese
 (1) completely remodelled their army, navy and education.
 (2) built up a German-type army.
 (3) were accepted by the great powers as equals.
 (4) made a modern navy with British help.

A Japanese naval victory during the Russian-Japanese war of 1904–5. Russia was heavily defeated in the war.

The Dowager Empress Tzu-Hsi of China receives visiting American ladies. The Chinese rejected European ideas and interference.

4 *The right order* Write these out in the order in which they happened.

(a) The Japanese built a modern navy.
(b) The Chinese rebelled against the 'foreign devils'.
(c) The Opium War began.
(d) Commodore Perry persuaded the Japanese to open up trade.

5 *The main idea* Write out the one sentence which tells what you think is the main idea of this topic.

(a) China had a huge population and a vast empire.
(b) Britain beat the Chinese in the Opium War.
(c) Westerners forced the Chinese and Japanese to trade with them.
(d) After long resistance the Chinese and Japanese accepted western ideas.

6 Using all the information in this chapter write out the different ways in which the Chinese and Japanese reacted to European influence during the nineteenth century.

7 What were the causes and results of the Opium War?

> Part of the Emperor of China's reply to the envoy from George III asking for better trading relations. 'We need nothing from you. We have all things. We do not value strange or ingenious objects. The manufactures of your country are not of the slightest use to us.

8 Explain how Japan became a world power between 1853 and 1905. (Clues: Perry, emperor, education, army and navy, invasion, war)

9 Study the picture of the naval battle. Imagine you were either a Japanese or a Russian war correspondent. Write a report on the battle for your newspaper.

10 *Research:*
Compile a project on either:

(a) Mao Tse-Tung and the Chinese Communist Revolution
(b) The history of Japan since 1931.

8 India in the nineteenth century

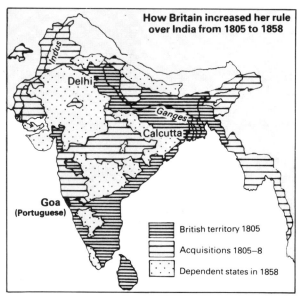

How Britain increased her rule over India from 1805 to 1858

	British territory 1805
	Acquisitions 1805–8
	Dependent states in 1858

How Britain increased her rule over India

The peoples of India are different in many ways from those of Europe. Their dress, customs and religion are based upon a very old civilization, far older than that of Britain. By the nineteenth century the Europeans, by their scientific approach, had developed new methods in medicine, industry and warfare, while the people of India still preferred their original old ways.

The result of this was that small numbers of British people were able to maintain and increase their power over the vast Indian population and territory. Soon after Clive had led the East India Company to victory over the Indian leaders who had been supported by the French, the British government passed the India Bill in 1784, giving the British government control of India. Most of the work of government however, was left to the East India Company.

There were many states in India ruled over by their princes. One by one, many of these were brought under British control. Some states were taken over completely; others were left under Indian rulers so long as they ruled in accordance with British wishes. There was armed rebellion in the Punjab, which resulted in it being taken over in 1849. When the British Governor General thought that the state of Oudh was being ruled badly, he took that over. Berar did not pay its debts, so that too became British. In Jaipur, Nagur and Jhansi the prince died without leaving an heir, so they were included in British India.

The British had first come to India to trade, and profitable trade was still their main object. In thousands of villages and in some large towns, many Indian people made cotton cloth on hand looms. In the early nineteenth century the British people were making huge quantities of cotton cloth on machines. The cotton manufacturers wanted British people to stop buying Indian cloth, so taxes were put on Indian cloth coming into Britain. Cheap British-made cloth, on the other hand, was allowed into India free of tax. As a result the Indian cloth makers could no longer sell their cloth. They were ruined. Many died of starvation; but the British cotton trade was thriving.

The British also believed that they had a duty to bring peace and good government to India. They were quite sure that their own way of life, their religion and their language were much better than those of the Indian people. Some British people went to India and gave up all their time and energy to improving the health of the people. Schools were started, but they taught the Indian boys, not in an Indian language, but in English. British missionaries tried to persuade the Indian people to become Christians.

Some Indian and some Christian religious customs

Some Indian religious customs seemed to the British to be very wrong. Lord Bentinck, the Governor General, stopped the custom of Suttee, by which widows burned themselves to death on their husbands' funeral pyres. He also stopped the Thugs, a society whose members strangled people for relgious reasons. He reduced the number of baby girls that were killed when they were not wanted. Some Indian people too thought these things were wrong, but they resented interference by the British. They knew that only a few years

An Indian prince, the Maharaja Raghurag Shingh of Rewah.

before this, children in England were being hanged for stealing a few pence, and that in the seventeenth century Christians had used horrible tortures, and burned one another to death for religious reasons.

Growing discontent

Lord Dalhousie, Governor General from 1848 to 1856, introduced many western ideas and methods, such as railways, the telegraph and a cheap postage service. Some Indians did not like the new ideas. Dislike and discontent grew, as it seemed to them that the British were ignoring or deliberately forcing them to break the Indian religious customs.

The British annoyed the Sepoys (Indian soldiers serving the British) by ignoring some of their religious ideas. The Sepoys were ordered to wear turbans and to trim their beards. Others were sent overseas without the special cooking utensils their religion demanded. Some Sepoys were Hindus to whom the cow was sacred, some were Moslems to whom the pig was unclean, so all were equally angry when they found that the cartridges for their rifles which they had to bite, were greased with the fat of cows and pigs. They considered it an insult to their religion, and refused to obey orders. The British hanged the leaders, or sentenced them to 900 lashes each. Others were given fourteen years hard labour on the roads.

It is not surprising that discontent grew, and in 1857 the Indian Mutiny broke out. Indian soldiers killed hundreds of British people. After hard fighting, the mutineers were defeated, and thousands of Indians, men, women and children were slaughtered in revenge.

The Indian Mutiny ended the governing power of the East India Company. In 1858 the Act for the Better Government of India was passed, putting the government of India completely in the hands of Parliament. Indian princes who had not already lost their lands to Britain were promised that the British army would protect them and keep them in power, so they became friendly to Britain. To make it easy to move troops about the country, and to keep order, and so make India a united country, thousands of kilometres of railways were constructed. These also helped trade. Harbours, canals and irrigation works also helped trade and improved food production, and lessened the risk of famine. Most of the money for these things was lent by British people, who were guaranteed that good interest on their money would be paid. If these things did not make enough profit to pay the interest, the Indian people were taxed to pay it, and in practice this meant that they had to send millions of pounds worth of goods to England without getting imports in return. At the same time the Indian people gained a transport system, and help in developing their own industries, and so were able to produce more food and other goods. Health was improved, and the population grew, but as most of the people were peasants, the increased population often meant a smaller holding of land for each, with the people remaining as poor as ever, and famines occurring frequently.

Educated Indians wanted to have a share in the government of their country. In 1885 they formed the Indian National Congress, to work for this; but long years of bitter feeling passed before they obtained their independence.

A European being carried in a palanquin by Indian bearers. The British especially asserted their superiority and with military support gained control of the sub-continent.

Exercises and things to do

A head covering and sun shade to protect Europeans against the Indian climate.

1 Write out, filling in the blanks. One – stands for each missing letter.

After the India Bill in 1784, the – – – – – – government controlled most of – – – – –. Some Indian states were left under – – – – – – rulers, but they had to rule as the – – – – – – – told them to.

Britain built up a big – – – – – with India, particularly in – – – – – – – – – – –, but many Indian – – – – – makers were ruined. The British also started – – – – – – –, and sent doctors and – – – – – – – – – – – –, to spread British ideas about – – – – – – and – – – – – – – –.

Many Indian people did not like British – – – – – – – – – – – in their – – – – – – – – and way of – – – –. There was a – – – – – – in 1857, and many people were killed. In 1885 the Indian – – – – – – – – – – – – – – – – – was formed to work for self- – – – – – – – – – – for the Indian people.

2 The heads and tails of these statements have been mixed. Write them out correctly.

(a) Clive	(1) introduced railways into India.
(b) Some Indian princes	(2) were Indian soldiers.
(c) Lord Dalhousie	(3) led the East India Company to victory.
(d) Sepoys	(4) were allowed to continue to rule.
(e) The cotton trade	(5) led to a demand for self government.
(f) The Indian National Congress	(6) brought profit to Britain, but ruin to many Indians.

Barrel organ in the shape of a man-eating tiger made for the ruler of Mysor in about 1790. The victim is a British East-India man.

3 *Statements of fact* Write out the four statements in each group in what you think is their order of importance or interest. Say in each group why you decided to put one particular statement first.

(a) The people of India differ from the British
   (1) in dress, religion, customs and language.
   (2) because they have an older civilization.
   (3) because most are not Christians.
   (4) in appearance.

(b) Britain increased her control of India
   (1) by taking over states that rebelled.
   (2) by annexing states that were ruled badly.
   (3) as a result of misrule, rebellion or lack of heirs.
   (4) when a ruler died without an heir.

(c) The British ruled India
   (1) to increase their trade.
   (2) to ensure peace, good government and prosperous British trade.
   (3) to convert the Indians to Christianity.
   (4) because they thought their way of life was better than that of the Indians.

4 *The right order* Write these out in the order in which they happened.

(a) The Indian Mutiny
(b) Indian cloth workers were ruined.
(c) The Indian National Congress was formed.
(d) The Punjab was annexed by Britain.

5 *The main idea* Choose the one sentence that tells what you think is the main idea of this topic.

(a) The Indians are different from the British people.
(b) British rule in India improved health, production and communication but did not satisfy the Indians.
(c) The Indian people became dissatisfied and began to work for independence.
(d) The British gradually took over more and more Indian territory.

6 Copy the map on page 32.

7 Outline the causes, course and consequences of the Indian Mutiny.

8 Design a poster to be displayed in Britain for men

   (a) to work as managers for the East India Company

or (b) to join the British Army in India

or (c) to act as engineers on the Darjeeling Railway.

9 Copy and complete this grid.

The British in India	
Disadvantages	Advantages
interference in Indian customs	*cheap postage service*

10 Why was the Indian National Congress formed?

'Agony Point' loop on the Darjeeling Railway. The British were responsible for the construction of Indian railways.

An advertisement for coffee essence. This was an easy way to make coffee. On later labels the sepoy, or Indian soldier, was shown as being less subservient.

British soldiers, administrators and merchants controlled nineteenth century India. Here, waited upon by Indian servants, British gentlemen and their ladies take tea.

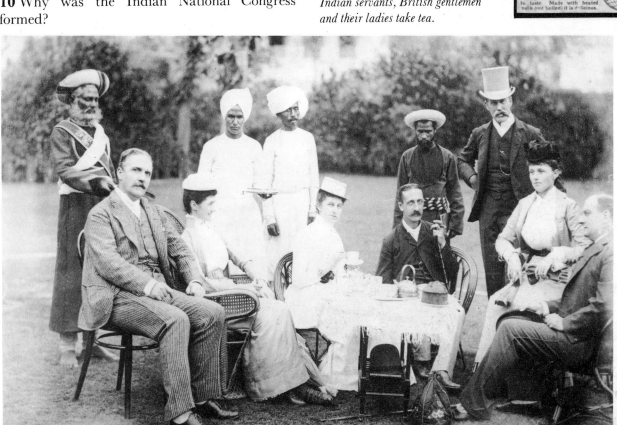

9 Changes in Europe

Empires and nations

In the middle of the nineteenth century there were two large empires in Europe – the Austrian and the Turkish. Each empire contained people of various nationalities who were increasingly anxious to gain the freedom to set up separate national states for themselves. At the same time there were two groups of states, each group containing members of the same nationality, but under separate rulers. These were the Italian and the German states. The people of the Italian states, most of which were ruled by Austrian, French or other foreigners, longed for a united Italy, ruled by Italian kings. In Germany the king of Prussia, the largest German state, hoped to unite the whole of Germany under his leadership.

Three leaders

The great prophet and inspirer of the Italian people to revolt against their foreign rulers was Mazzini. The statesman who worked for the unity of the Italian people was Cavour, and the hero of the struggle was Garibaldi.

Mazzini believed that the Italians themselves could gain freedom for Italy. He organized the society called Young Italy, which made several unsuccessful attempts at revolution in Savoy, Milan and Florence. In 1849 he was elected a leader of the new Roman Republic, but the republic was suppressed. He helped to organize risings in Milan in 1853 and Piedmont in 1857, and the invasion of Sicily in 1860. Unlike many Italians, he wanted, not an Italian king, but a republic.

Cavour was a statesman rather than a revolutionary, and he believed that the way to obtain a free Italy was to obtain the help of other kings and governments. He persuaded Napoleon III of France to support Piedmont against the Austrians, and in 1859 they were driven from Lombardy, which was added to the kingdom of Piedmont. The first stage in the uniting of Italy was accomplished.

Garibaldi was an enthusiastic follower of Mazzini. In 1860 the people of Sicily asked for help against their king, Ferdinand II. Garibaldi raised 1000 volunteers – the Red Shirts – and sailed to attack the 124,000 troops of Ferdinand. He smuggled on board some boxes labelled 'books'. They were filled with rifles.

The peasants joined Garibaldi, and he led them in a series of fierce batttles among the mountains. In three months he gained control of all Sicily. He crossed to the mainland, and after one battle, was master of the whole of southern Italy. In 1861 Victor Emmanuel of Piedmont took the title of King of Italy, with Cavour as his Prime Minister.

In 1866 Austria was defeated by Prussia, and Venice was taken from her and added to Italy. Four years later Rome, the last part of Italy to be freed from foreign rulers, joined the united kingdom of Italy when the French troops withdrew from the city.

Garibaldi, the military hero in the struggle for Italian unity and independence.

Germany

For hundreds of years the German people were divided into a large number of small states, some ruled by kings, some by princes, some by bishops. Napoleon Bonaparte swept away the boundaries between many of the smaller ones, but in the early nineteenth century there were still thirty-nine states. They tended to form into two groups: those in the north under the leadership of Prussia, while the south Germans looked to Austria for leadership. But many Germans, both north and south, felt that they were weak as a nation because they were so divided. They looked forward to a united Germany which would make the Germans strong and respected in Europe. Some of the rulers, however, were not anxious to see their power swallowed up by a German emperor.

The uniting of the Germans was very largely the work of one man – Prince Otto von Bismarck. In 1862 he became prime minister of Prussia, the largest north German state. He determined to unite all the Germans under the leadership of the king of Prussia. The first step was to displace Austria from the position she claimed as leader of the German people. Bismarck asked Austria for help in a war with Denmark, and then picked a quarrel with her over the terms of the treaty.

War: Prussia v Austria

Austria had been one of the great powers for centuries, and few people expected that Prussia would stand much chance of defeating her. Bismarck, however, had reorganized the Prussian army, and gained the support of many of the north German states. He struck at Austria's allies, and in three days took the capitals of Hanover and Saxony. He advanced into Austria with great speed, and completely defeated the Austrians at Königgratz. In six weeks the war was over.

Prussia then took over any small north German

In 1870 the Prussians surrounded Paris. Napoleon III surrendered and France was humiliated. Here Parisians look through telescopes at the besieging Prussian troops.

states that had supported Austria, and formed all the northern German states into the North German Federation. Bismarck had then to persuade the southern German states to accept the leadership of Prussia. They were not at all anxious to do so, but Bismarck guessed that fear of France could be used to persuade them.

There was ill feeling between Prussia and France, and in 1870 Bismarck goaded Napoleon III of France into declaring war on Prussia. Bismarck made this appear to be an attack upon all Germans, and the south rallied to Prussia's support. The Prussian army quickly advanced into France. On 2 September 1870, Napoleon was forced to surrender with his army at Sedan. By 1871 France was utterly defeated, and forced to surrender the provinces of Alsace and Lorraine to Germany, and to pay a large indemnity.

The German empire

All the German states were then united in the German empire, with King William I of Prussia as the first emperor of Germany. Bismarck did all he could to keep France as weak and isolated as possible. In 1879 he formed an alliance with Austria, and three years later he brought Italy into the alliance, which was called the Triple Alliance. Bismarck did his best to keep on friendly terms with Russia, to prevent her, if possible, from becoming an ally of France. But Russia and Britain were worried that Germany was becoming dangerously strong. All the main countries of Europe increased the size and power of their armies and navies. 'If you want peace,' the people of Europe were told, 'prepare for war.' What they got was the First World War in 1914.

Exercises and things to do

1 Write out, filling in the blanks. One – stands for each missing letter.

In the mid nineteenth century Germany consisted of many separate ––––––, of which –––––– was the largest. The Italians were in several states which were ruled by ––––––––––. Three men helped the Italians to –––––. –––––– formed Young –––––, and led several attempts at ––––––––––. Then –––––– got the –––––– to help to drive out the Austrians. In 1860 –––––––––– led the people of –––––– and all southern ––––– in a successful fight, and most of the country formed a united –––––– of –––––.

In Germany, ––––––––, Prime Minister of Prussia defeated the –––––––– and united the northern ––––– states, and then, after defeating –––––, united all the German states in the –––––– empire.

2 The heads and tails of these statements have been mixed. Write them out correctly.

(a) Prussia	(1) was the leader of the south German states.
(b) Mazzini	(2) became prime minister of the kingdom of Italy.
(c) Cavour	(3) organized Young Italy.
(d) Bismarck	(4) led the struggle in southern Italy.
(e) Garibaldi	(5) was the prime minister of Prussia.
(f) Austria	(6) was the largest north German state.

Nine of the European monarchs who attended the funeral of King Edward VII in 1910. On this photograph are the kings of England, Germany, Norway, Bulgaria, Portugal, Greece, Belgium and Spain. Seated in the middle is King George V of England and behind him is his cousin, Kaiser Wilhelm II of Germany. They were cousins of Czar Nicholas of Russia.

3 *Statements of fact* Write out the four statements in each group in the order of importance or interest. Say in each group why you decided to put one particular statement first.

(a) In the mid nineteenth century
  (1) the Austrian Empire contained many subject peoples.
  (2) the Italian people wanted unity.
  (3) there were thirty-nine states in Germany.
  (4) the spirit of nationalism made the Germans long for unity.

(b) In Italy
  (1) Mazzini inspired Italian patriots by founding Young Italy.
  (2) Cavour wanted to unite Italy under the King of Piedmont.
  (3) Cavour gained Lombardy with the help of Napoleon III.
  (4) Garibaldi added Sicily and southern Italy to united Italy.

(c) Prince Otto von Bismarck
  (1) became prime minister of Prussia in 1862.
  (2) was the creator of a united Germany.
  (3) wanted to make Prussia the leader of all the German states.
  (4) led Prussia in the defeat of Austria and France.

4 *The right order* Write these out in the order in which they happened.

(a) Bismarck became prime minister of Prussia.
(b) The Battle of Sedan.
(c) Garibaldi freed Sicily.
(d) The formation of the Triple Alliance.

5 *The main idea* Write out the one sentence which tells what you think is the main idea of this topic.

(a) Each nation in Europe wanted its own state with all its own people in it.
(b) By wars with Austria and France Bismarck united the German states.
(c) Bismarck formed the Triple Alliance.
(d) The spirit of nationalism led to the unification of Italy.

6 Show how Mazzini, Cavour and Garibaldi brought about the unification and independence of Italy.

7 Look at the picture of Kaiser Wilhelm II. Which parts of it indicate Germany's wish to become a more powerful nation?

8 Using other books either write a biography of Bismarck or compile a project on the France/Prussian War.

Kaiser Wilhelm II (1859–1941) 1 Under the left eye: 2 June 1880 – betrothal to Princess Augusta Victoria. 2 Under the right eye: airship Zeppelin and biplane. 3 Chin and moustache: 10 August 1890 – invasion of island of Heligoland by the Kaiser. 4 Right cheek: 1 January 1891 – Raising of the German war flag on the East African coast. 5 Collar: 21 June 1895 – opening of the Kiel canal. 6 Right temple: 2 June 1899 – naming of the cruiser 'Kaiser Wilhelm the Great.' 7 Brow: 2 July 1900 – Dispatching a division to East Asia; Kaiser's farewell to the soldiers. 8 Above the brow: Kaiser Parade. 9 Ear: Hohenzollern yacht.

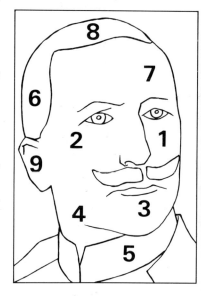

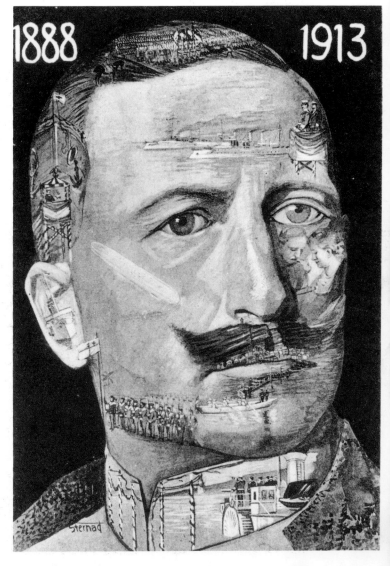

Science in everyday life

1 What advantages did Yates, Haywood and Co. claim for their gas stove? Describe how people may have cooked before gas ovens were invented (*clue:* fire) and then either collect pictures to show how cookers have changed, or copy the Rotherham gas stove and beside it draw a modern stove.

THE
ROTHERHAM GAS STOVE
(PATENTED).

The only Stove that Boils and Roasts at same time.

COOKS SEVEN DINNERS FOR 2d.

PRICE **15/-** (GROSS).

YATES, HAYWOOD & CO.,
And the Rotherham Foundry Co., Lim.,
ROTHERHAM and LONDON.

3 Make a list of the advantages that a sewing machine would have for a large family with both parents working.

2 Imagine that you are a domestic maid servant and that your mistress has bought a vacuum cleaner. Write a letter to your family describing the new cleaner and saying how it saves you time and effort.

A flush toilet. The cistern was made of mahogany and lined with copper. This model cost £10.

4 A washing machine of 1874. It cost £6. What advantages does a modern washing machine have over the 1874 model?

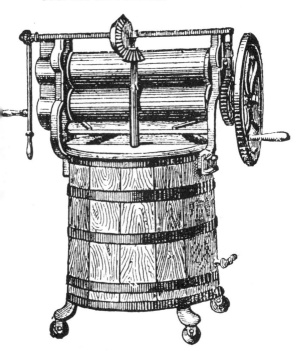

5 Using this picture design an advertisement for a disc gramophone. The cost is £3. Use these ideas: music, voice, clear sound, home entertainment.

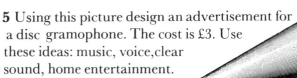

6 List the items stored in the refrigerator. Of what value to the home was such a gadget?

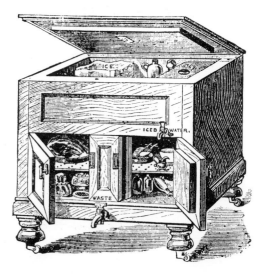

7 A radio of the 1930s. Compile an illustrated project showing how radios have changed over the past fifty years.

8 The first television picture in London. How do you think television has affected (a) newspapers (b) radio (c) live sport (d) the theatre and cinema.

10 Empire building: the new British empire

In 1776 Britain's American colonies revolted, and declared their independence. After that, many British people began to wonder whether colonies were worth having. If colonists were going to break away as soon as they were prosperous, why trouble to have colonies at all? The British government certainly was not anxious to replace the lost American colonies by developing new ones. Nevertheless, the foundations of a vast new realm of empire had already been laid. The man responsible was Captain James Cook.

James Cook was the son of a farm labourer. He did not go regularly to school, and learned only a little writing and arithmetic, but he read any books he could get. He worked on a coal ship, and learned a great deal about navigation. He joined the navy as an able seaman in 1755. He very soon rose to the position of boatswain. He was sent to North America during the war with the French. He had taught himself trigonometry, and was an expert at chart-making. He charted the river St Lawrence, and so gave vital help to General Wolfe in the capture of Quebec in 1759.

In 1768, Cook was chosen to command an expedition to the south Pacific. This map shows his explorations. He claimed the whole of eastern Australia for Britain.

Although the newly discovered lands had been claimed for Britain, the British government did nothing about them for some time, and no colonists sailed at once to take possession; but events in America brought a change. Convicts had often been sent from Britain to the North American colonies to work in the plantations. When the colonies became independent, this was no longer possible, and the British government found a use for the new lands Cook had discovered for them – they could dump their convicts there. Thus the great Dominion of Australia began in 1788 with a settlement of 750 convicts at Port Jackson, near the modern Sydney.

The convicts were not by any means all bad men. Some were those who had spirit enough to poach for their starving families from the game preserves of the rich landowners, or to try to form trade unions when these were illegal. These men often made excellent citizens after they had served their term. Soon free settlers also arrived in Australia. Gradually one of Britain's greatest colonies was created.

The British government was even slower in taking advantage of Captain Cook's other main exploration. Although New Zealand was fertile, with a pleasant climate very suitable for British

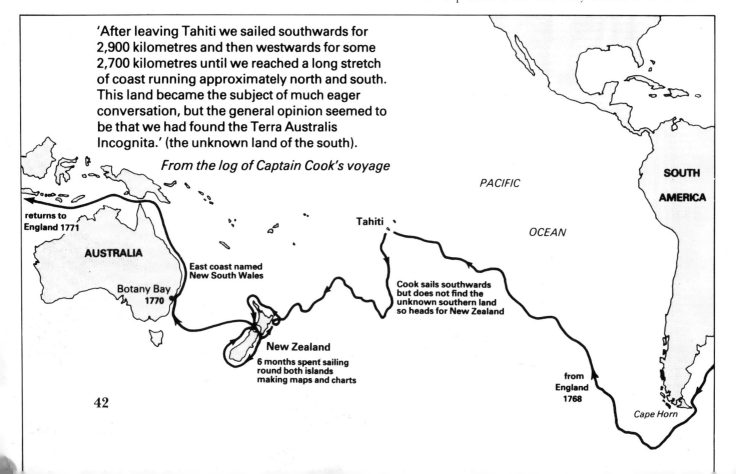

'After leaving Tahiti we sailed southwards for 2,900 kilometres and then westwards for some 2,700 kilometres until we reached a long stretch of coast running approximately north and south. This land became the subject of much eager conversation, but the general opinion seemed to be that we had found the Terra Australis Incognita.' (the unknown land of the south).

From the log of Captain Cook's voyage

returns to England 1771

AUSTRALIA

East coast named New South Wales

Botany Bay 1770

New Zealand
6 months spent sailing round both islands making maps and charts

Tahiti

Cook sails southwards but does not find the unknown southern land so heads for New Zealand

PACIFIC

OCEAN

SOUTH AMERICA

from England 1768

Cape Horn

settlers, more than sixty years passed before the New Zealand Company was formed to settle the land. Then another important British colony came into being.

Although British governments were not anxious to obtain new or larger colonies, the British empire continued to grow, mainly because individuals were pressing on into the unknown to explore, to find land to settle or to take futher land to protect lands which were already settled from warlike raids. The native peoples, such as the American Indians in Canada, and the Australian aborigines or Blackfellows were largely driven from their home and land, and much reduced in numbers.

Canada

In Canada there were two colonies, Upper and Lower Canada, one of which contained many French colonists. In each, the colonists elected an Assembly, but it had little power, and most of the government was in the hands of the governor who was sent out from Britain. In 1837 there were rebellions in both colonies, and Lord Durham was sent to look into things. He suggested that all the people of Canada should be united in one colony with a parliament which should make its own laws. This was done during the next twenty-seven years. The huge country was divided into several provinces, and these were combined in 1867 into the Dominion of Canada. The Canadian Parliament controlled everything except foreign affairs.

In 1871 British Columbia in the far west joined the Dominion, and the Canadian Pacific Railway was built to link it with the rest of Canada. Wheat growing, lumbering, mining and manufacturing developed, and from a colony, Canada grew into a separate nation, and was known as a self-governing dominion. In the twentieth century it

A Chinese labour gang working on the construction of the Canadian Pacific Railway at Glacier Park, British Columbia (1889).

was given the right to conduct its own foreign affairs, and Canada became truly independent.

Meanwhile in Australia, from Sydney, Melbourne, Brisbane, Adelaide and Perth, settlers pressed inland. For some time many of the settlers were convicts, but increasing numbers of free immigrants arrived. Sheep were raised and gold mined. Trade with Britain increased rapidly, as the factories of Britain needed more and more wool for the manufacture of cloth.

In New Zealand the company formed in 1840 to take over the islands met with fierce resistance from the Maori inhabitants, who fought to try to keep their lands and way of life. When at last they were defeated, they were treated as good citizens, and given the same rights as the white settlers, and allowed to send members to the House of Representatives, the New Zealand Parliament.

A native offering a fish to a member of Cook's crew. Cook discovered much about the Pacific Ocean and its island peoples. His scientific discoveries were also of great value.

Exercises and things to do

1 Write out, filling in the blanks. One – stands for each missing letter.

Captain James Cook was sent in the year ———— to explore the great ———————— Ocean, and the little-known lands there. He sailed round the two islands of ——— ———————, making careful ——————, and then went on to eastern ——————————. He claimed all ——————— Australia for Britain, and called it ——— ————— —————. At first the British government did nothing about it, but after the ———————— colonies became the ———, Britain could no longer send her ———————— there, so in ————, 750 of them were sent to ——————————. Later ———— settlers joined them, and gradually the whole of —————————— became a ——————— colony. New ——————— was not made a colony until ————. Many settlers went to Canada which was made a ———————— in ————, with its own ——————————.

2 The heads and tails of this statements have been mixed. Write them out correctly.

(a) The Maoris	(1) were the native people of Australia.
(b) Tasman	(2) made the first exploration of the east coast of Australia.
(c) New South Wales	(3) was the name given to western Canada.
(d) The Blackfellows	(4) were the people of New Zealand.
(e) James Cook	(5) was the first European to visit New Zealand.
(f) British Columbia	(6) was the name Cook gave to eastern Australia.

3 *Statements of fact* Write out the four statements in each group in what you think is their order of importance or interest. Say in each group why you decided to put one particular statement first.

(a) Australia
   (1) had a pleasant fertile eastern coast.
   (2) became a convict settlement.
   (3) produced sheep and gold for trade with Britain.
   (4) grew into a great dominion of the British empire.

(b) New Zealand
   (1) was explored and charted by Captain Cook.
   (2) was inhabited by Maoris.
   (3) was settled mainly after 1840.
   (4) became a dominion with Maoris in its parliament.

(c) Canada
   (1) contained many French colonists.
   (2) was made of several provinces which in 1867 formed the Dominion of Canada.
   (3) grew from a colony into a self-governing dominion.
   (4) developed wheat growing, lumbering, mining and manufacturing.

4 *The right order* Write these out in the order in which they happened.

(a) The New Zealand Company was formed.
(b) the first convict settlers arrived in Australia.
(c) Cook explored the east coast of Australia.
(d) Canada became a dominion.

The painted face of a Maori, a native of New Zealand. Cook's journals contained information about many aspects of life in the South Pacific. His maps and charts were invaluable to later sailors.

5 *The main idea* Write down the one sentence which tells what you think is the main idea of this topic.

(a) Cook laid the foundations for a new British empire.

(b) From a convict settlement Australia grew to be a self-governing dominion.

(c) During the nineteenth century Britain made several new colonies which developed parliaments of their own.

(d) Britain built up a large trade with her colonies.

6 Imagine you were the British Prime Minister in 1783. Write to King George III pointing out the value of Australia as a convict colony.

7 Draw a strip cartoon of ten scenes called 'Transportation to Australia'.

8 What is the difference between a colony and a dominion?

9 (a) On an outline map of Canada mark in the major towns and the route of the Canadian Pacific Railway.

(b) On an outline map of Australia mark in the major towns, the gold producing areas, and the sheep rearing areas.

After the loss of the American colonies Britain sent convicts to Australia. In 1788 Captain Arthur Phillip arrived at Port Jackson with six ships and 750 convicts. This sketch of 1842 shows a chain gang going to work.

In the 1850s gold was discovered in New South Wales and Victoria. Gold diggers streamed to Ballarat and Bendigo. Later, gold was found in Queensland and Western Australia.

10 *Project*
Compile an illustrated biography of Captain James Cook.

In 1797 Captain John MacArthur imported Spanish merino sheep into Australia and began the country's greatest industry — sheep rearing. Here sheep shearers pose at Canowie, South Australia.

11 The scramble for empire

Several European countries have built up empires by the conquest of foreign peoples and the seizing of their land. Spain and Portugal built up big empires in the sixteenth century; Holland, Britain, and France in the seventeenth and eighteenth centuries. Portugal lost much of her empire to the Dutch, and the French lost some of theirs to the British. Early in the nineteenth century the American colonies of Spain and Portugal gained their independence, and again it appeared to many people that colonies were not worth having, so throughout the greater part of the nineteenth century, most of the European countries were not anxious to gain new colonies. Bismarck, the prime minister of Prussia, said that a colony was not worth the bones of a single German soldier.

About 1880 a great change took place in the attitude towards colonies. The growing industries in Europe led to an increase in the need for all sorts of raw materials, such as rubber and vegetable oils. Fresh markets were also needed for the manufactures. It was hoped that colonies would provide both of these. As steamships increased the speed and volume of trade, and the railways made it possible to open up ways into the interior, new trading stations were established. Then expeditions from the trading stations pushed inland, and claims to vast new colonies were staked out. Countries now felt that colonies added not only to their wealth, but to their importance in the world. Germany joined in this new scramble for empire. Within a few years almost the whole of Africa was shared out between Britain, France, Germany, Italy, Spain, Portugal and Belgium. There was intense rivalry between Britain and Germany, France and Italy, and Britain and France.

There was so much land to be seized, however, that war was avoided, and the rivalry largely consisted in a race to get native chiefs to sign treaties giving away their territory to European governments or trading companies, in exchange for 'protection' and a few hundred pounds or an old river steamer. In the Cameroons the British arrived just five days after the Germans had made a treaty with the natives. The French arrived six days later. In Nigeria the Germans sailing up the river Niger met the British sailing down with their treaty just signed. Bismarck called a conference in 1884 to settle the division of the African spoils.

'One in the eye for King Umberto' A cartoon mocking the Italian defeat by the Ethiopians at Makalle in 1896. European nations delighted in the defeat of another.

China

In China the Europeans claimed the right to take over Chinese ports, where Europeans lived under their own laws. They administered the customs and operated railways which were built to help their trade with China. Chinese protests were put down by force. Japan joined the western powers in exploiting China, seizing Korea and Formosa. Russia took some of China's northern territory, while France took Indo-China which had once owed allegiance to China.

The islands of the Pacific were shared out between the colonial powers, so that by 1900 almost the whole world except most of the Americas was ruled or largely controlled by Europeans. Some parts such as the British dominions were given a good deal of power to govern themselves, some were allowed to elect an advisory council, and many were under the absolute rule of a European governor. Some were inhabited mainly by white people, some by African or Asiatic peoples, some by a complicated mixture of races, religions and colours. These far-flung parts of the empires were linked by European navies and by innumerable trading vessels.

The demand in some colonies for self-government continued, and where most of the people were white some steps were taken to satisfy this. In Australia, separate colonies had formed round the main settlements, and in 1900 they combined to form a self-governing dominion of the British empire. In South Africa war broke out in 1899 between the British and the Boers, the descendants of the original Dutch colonists. After long, hard fighting the Boers were defeated, but in 1909 Boer and British colonists joined to form the Dominion of the Union of South Africa.

46

Getting rid of the unwanted

During the nineteenth century wages in many parts of Europe were low, and there was often much unemployment. In Britain workers were encouraged by the government and by trade unions to emigrate to the colonies. From the early seventeenth century emigration had been a way of getting rid of unwanted people. On the other hand, it was considered a bad thing to lose good workers, and there were laws to prevent skilled craftsmen from leaving the country.

After 1815 when there was often no work for the soldiers discharged from the army after the wars with Napoleon, the government offered very cheap passages to Canada. In 1824 the restrictions on the emigration of skilled workers were abolished. Parish authorities also organized schemes for getting rid of their unemployed by sending them abroad. During the 1830s emigrants averaged 50,000 a year, and by 1900 this had risen to 200,000. Most British emigrants went to the USA, Canada, Australia and New Zealand.

Other people besides the British wanted to emigrate to Australia, but the Australians decided to keep theirs a white people's country, so coloured people were not allowed to live and work there. The Australians feared that people from countries such as Japan and India would be willing to work for much lower wages, and to sell goods at much lower prices, which would not be good for Australian workers and shopkeepers.

'From the Cape to Cairo' The telegraph link between South Africa and Egypt was only part of Cecil Rhodes's dream to establish total British control of Africa.

The Japanese, with a population of nearly eighty millions looked with jealous eyes at the vast land of Australia, which had barely eight million people. They thought the policy of 'White Australia' unfair.

The Americans allowed a constant stream of immigrants, mainly Irish, German and Scandinavian, to flow into the USA. The Irish provided the manpower for the building up of industry, and the construction of canals and railroads. The population of Ireland which had been over eight million earlier in the nineteenth century, fell to four and half million after a famine had driven many of them to emigrate.

The Chinese provided the labour for the railroads in the far west of the USA, until the government took alarm at the rapidly increasing number of Chinese, and in 1885 severely limited the number of new Chinese immigrants.

Meanwhile a new flood of immigrants was flowing into America from eastern and southern Europe. The government became alarmed. Americans had claimed that their country was a great 'melting pot' which fused the different European immigrant peoples into one great American nation. Now it appeared that it was not so successful after all. In 1924 almost all of certain types of immigration was stopped.

Britain, Germany and Russia, watched by France, discuss the division of China. European nations were portrayed as stereotypes in contemporary cartoons.

47

Exercises and things to do

1 Write out, filling in the blanks. One – stands for each missing letter.

In the sixteenth century big empires were built up by ––––– and ––––––––, and in the seventeenth and eighteenth centuries by ––––––, ––––––––, and ––––––. When some of these colonies had gained their –––––––––––, most European countries wondered whether –––––––– were worth having; but about the year ––––, things changed, and some countries thought colonies would be very valuable for –––––. Almost all –––––– was shared out between them. Some ports in ––––– were taken over, and some parts of the –––––– empire were seized by ––––––, –––––– and –––––.

2 The heads and tails of these sentences have been mixed. Write them out correctly.

(a) Immigrants	(1) seized Korea from China.
(b) The Japanese	(2) streamed into the USA.
(c) The 'melting pot'	(3) was how Australians described their country.
(d) The Cameroons	(4) became a British colony.
(e) Nigeria	(5) became a German colony.
(f) The white people's country	(6) was the name given to the USA.

3 *Statements of fact* Write out the four statements in each group in what you think is their order of importance or interest. Say in each group why you decided to put one particular statement first.

(a) After 1815 emigration from London and other British ports
   (1) was encouraged because discharged soldiers were without jobs.
   (2) was helped by the offer of cheap passages to Canada.
   (3) averaged 50,000 in the 1830s.
   (4) increased steadily from 20,000 in the 1820s to 200,000 in 1900.

(b) Immigration into the USA
   (1) increased throughout the nineteenth century.
   (2) was open to all peoples until 1885.
   (3) brought increasing numbers from Europe who did much to build the American nation.
   (4) was severely limited after 1924.

(c) Towards the end of the nineteenth century
   (1) Germany began to acquire colonies.
   (2) European countries began a great scramble for colonies.
   (3) railways opened up ways into the interior of countries which could be colonized.
   (4) industrial countries wanted easy access to more raw materials.

4 *The right order* Write these out in the order in which they happened.

(a) The USA restricted immigration of the Chinese.
(b) The British government offered cheap passages to Canada.
(c) The conference of Berlin settled the share-out of Africa.
(d) The war with the Boers broke out.

The scramble for Africa

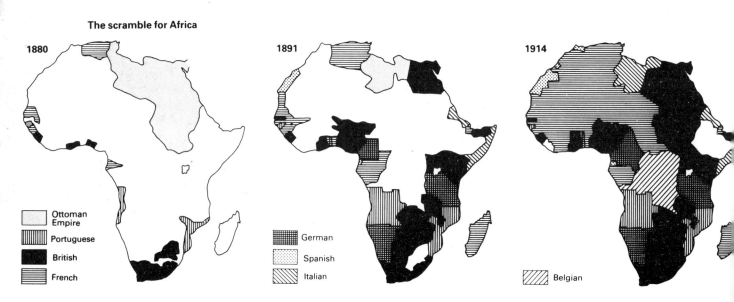

1880   1891   1914

Ottoman Empire
Portuguese
British
French
German
Spanish
Italian
Belgian

5 *The main idea* Write out the sentence which tells what you think is the main idea of this topic.

(a) Emigration from Europe to the USA and the dominions increased throughout the nineteenth century.
(b) Emigration helped to solve unemployment in Europe and built up new countries overseas.
(c) Between 1880 and 1914 most of the world except America was shared out between Europeans.
(d) There was a scramble for colonies in the late nineteenth century.

6 How is each European nation represented on the cartoon on page 46?

7 Write a paragraph explaining why European nations competed for imperial possessions.

8 Using the maps on page 48 and a modern atlas compile lists of those African countries governed by Britain, France, Belgium, Italy and Germany.

9 Imagine that as a young person you left England to live in one of the colonies. Write a letter to a friend or relative to tell them of your experiences. (Clues: no job in England, sea journey, first impressions, job, climate, etc.)

10 Choose one of the following countries – India, New Zealand, Jamaica, Canada, Kenya, Pakistan, Australia and South Africa. Collect pictures and information about its people.

A Nigerian king and his entourage wear a mixture of native and European clothes. Europeans had influence in more important aspects of life.

11 *Research project*
Either: (a) Write a biography of Cecil Rhodes.
or (b) Compile a project on the Boer war (1899–1902).

One of the more destructive forms of Western technology introduced to Africa was the gun. Although native armies did win battles they had little chance against weapons such as the maxim gun.

12 The United States of America

The United States of America was a new sort of country. It not only ended the idea held by many Europeans that they could take any part of the world for their own use, and enslave other peoples, but it was based on the Declaration of Independence, which said that all people were born with equal rights. In the USA there were to be no kings, lords and earls; their Parliament had no House of Lords. There were two parts to their Parliament, the Senate and the House of Representatives, but all members of both houses were elected by the people. The thirteen colonies which had carried out the revolution were the states of the USA, and as more land was developed, more states were created. Each state had its own government for local affairs, while matters of war and peace, and the main laws and taxes were decided by the central government. A President of the whole country was elected by the people. A Supreme Court of leading judges checked that all laws passed were in agreement with the ideas stated in the Declaration of Independence, on which the whole country's government was based.

The spread of American ideas

There was no attempt to force all the people to adopt one religion, or to prevent people who believed in any particular religion from holding important positions, as had been the case in most European countries. The French and other European kings who had helped the American colonists to gain their freedom from Britain did not realize how dangerous the American ideas could be to themselves: within a dozen years France, the country of the 'Great King' was in the midst of violent revolution.

American ideas of revolution also spread to the colonies of Spain and Portugal in America, and they began to fight for their freedom. When several European countries suggested joining together to help Spain to suppress the revolts,

President Monroe of the USA warned them that any interference in any part of America would be regarded as an act of war against the USA. Within a few years, from Mexico southwards, almost all the colonies had become independent countries.

An expanding USA

Meanwhile the USA was growing steadily westwards. The huge area of Louisiana was bought from the French, and the first steamboat was launched on the Mississippi, which made easy access into the heart of the continent. From there, in covered wagons to carry their families and stores, the pioneers pressed along the Oregon, Santa Fé and California trails, across the vast prairie plains, and over range after range of mountains until at last those who had not died from thirst, starvation and Indian attacks reached the fertile lands of the far west.

Slavery

For a long time after the foundation of the USA there were still slaves in many parts of the country. The right to freedom laid down in the Declaration of Independence did not yet apply to them. Many people depended almost entirely upon the work of slaves. In the north most of the people worked in manufacturing, or were farmers using methods like those in Britain, and these did not need slave labour, but in the south were great estates on which multitudes of slaves toiled under burning sun in cotton fields and tobacco plantations for their white masters. As each new state was formed, it had to decide whether it would be a free or a slave state.

In 1833 an American anti-slavery society was formed in the north, which wanted to abolish slavery completely, but they were bitterly opposed by the people of the south. The unity of the USA was threatened. Members of the anti-slavery society went into the slave states to urge that slavery should be ended. The slave owners were very angry at these interfering northerners. They said slaves were happier than workers in the north who toiled for long hours in bad conditions in factories and were often unemployed. The slaves were well treated, and protected from unemployment. Northerners helped runaway slaves to

Slave poster

escape to the north. When the northerners said there must be no further spread of slavery, the southerners talked about breaking away from the Union, unless it was agreed that slavery could be extended to the Pacific. President Lincoln would not agree to this, and the southern states decided to form a separate, slave-owning Union. They began seizing forts and stores. To Lincoln, the question of preserving the unity of the country was vital, and he was ready to fight to maintain it. Thus the American Civil War began.

The War and after

Before the war ended, nearly 2,000,000 men were taking part, and the war swayed backwards and forwards across the country, with terrible loss of life and waste of wealth. Lincoln encouraged the people of the north, and in a famous speech he said 'We here highly resolve that these dead shall not have died in vain, that this nation, under God, shall have a new birth of freedom, and that government of the people, by the people and for the people, shall not perish from the earth.'

The north won the war, and just as Lincoln was hoping to make a peace settlement to draw the two sides together, he was shot dead.

The negroes in the south were given the right to vote, and many of the whites lost theirs. To cope with the wrecked cities, the plantations which had been laid waste, and the ruined trade proved too difficult for the negroes, and gradually the whites regained control, and the negroes lost many of their rights. Meanwhile the north had grown prosperous. Oil and gold had been discovered, new factories and railways had been built. In 1869 the first railway from the Atlantic to the Pacific was completed. Soon China was brought into close touch with eastern USA: in thirty days the tea and rich silks of China were in New York.

Immigrants came pouring into the United States, and along the railways to the west. Huge ranches, and then vast wheat fields covered the prairies, and great quantities of food began to cross the Atlantic to Europe. European farmers, particularly British, found cheap food from America was threatening them with serious loss. Meanwhile vast fortunes were being built up in the USA. In 1860 there were three millionaires there; in 1900 there were four thousand.

All was not perfect in the American system: in 1873 there was panic in the business world, many banks closed their doors, many firms crashed in bankruptcy, hundreds of thousands of men were thrown out of work. In 1877 there was a great

From cotton fields to cotton thread. A nineteenth century advertisement showing the various stages in the production of cotton.

railway strike, and troops were called out to break it. In 1886 the American Federation of Labour was formed, but a few years later armed guards shot down its members who were striking. But despite these troubles, the USA, with its great size and resources, appeared to the rest of the world, to be the land of hope and opportunity.

51

The United States of America

Exercises and things to do

1 Write out the following, filling in the blanks. One – stands for each missing letter.

The USA was a different country from most of Europe. There were no –––––, ––––– and –––––. The –––––––––– of –––––––––––– stated that all men were born with ––––– rights. Their Parliament had ––– parts, the –––––– and the House of –––––––––––––––. All members of both were ––––––– by the people.
    Other colonies copied the USA and began to fight for their –––––––. Then President –––––– of the USA warned the –––––––– countries not to –––––––– in any –––– of –––––––.
    A dispute between the northern and –––––––– states about the spread of––––––– led to a ––––– –––. President ––––––– led the –––––––– states to prevent the South from –––––––– away from the –––––.

2 The heads and tails of these statements have been mixed. Write them out correctly.

(a) The Senate   (1) was made up of important judges.
(b) President Monroe   (2) led the north in the civil war.
(c) The Anti-slavery Society (3) was mainly to keep the USA united.
(d) The Supreme Court (4) was part of the American Parliament.
(e) The American Civil War (5) aimed at ending slavery in the USA.
(f) President Lincoln (6) told Europeans not to interfere in any part of America.

3 *Statements of fact* Write out the four statements in each group, in what you think is their order of importance or interest. Say in each group why you decided to put one particular statement first.

(a) The USA government
    (1) was headed by a president.
    (2) had a Parliament of two parts.
    (3) had no kings, lords or earls.
    (4) was based upon the Declaration of Independence.

(b) The American Civil War
    (1) began when the southern states decided to break away from the union.
    (2) led to an end to slavery in the United States.
    (3) was won by the north.
    (4) led to terrible loss of life and waste of wealth.

4 *The right order* Write these out in the order in which they happened.

(a) The first railway right across the USA was completed.
(b) The American Civil War broke out.
(c) The Declaration of Independence was drawn up.
(d) Ideas of revolution spread to other colonies in America.

5 *The main idea* Write out the one sentence which tells what you think is the main idea of this topic.

(a) The USA grew up as a result of the Declaration of Independence.
(b) The USA grew from a few colonies to become a rich and powerful nation.
(c) Civil war, business panics and strikes in which leaders were shot down all happened in the USA.
(d) The USA provided work for huge numbers of immigrants from Europe.

6 Copy and colour the picture of the Indian Chief.

7 Copy and colour the map on page 52. On the map mark in New York, Boston, Washington DC, Dallas, Houston, Chicago, San Francisco and Philadelphia.

8 Between 1840 and 1910 twenty-six million immigrants entered the United States. List the advantages and disadvantages of this immigration.

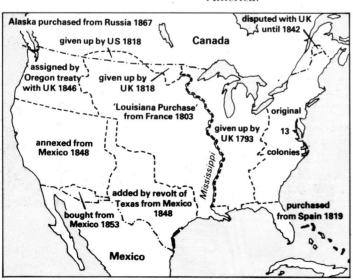

How the USA expanded from 1776 to 1867

President Abraham Lincoln tried to prevent the extension of slavery and the break up of the USA. He led the northern armies to victory but was assassinated in April 1865.

Shooting buffalo on the track of the Kansas Pacific Railway, 1871. The slaughter of the buffalo deprived the Indians of their livelihood because they relied upon the animal for so many things.

A sketch by Karl Bodmer of an Indian chief. The Indians used the animals and birds they hunted for food, clothing and weapons. Despite their brave resistance they were no match for the invading white man.

The United States of America was a haven for the unwanted and oppressed peoples of Europe. Over 8000 immigrants a day passed through Ellis Island, New York, in the 1900s.

9 Describe in detail what you can see on the advertisement on page 51.

10 Look at the flag of the United States. What do the stars and stripes represent?

11 Using other library books either:

(a) Write a short biography of Abraham Lincoln

or (b) Compile a project on the American Civil War.

13 The First World War

Smiling French troops leave for the battlefront in August 1914. Part of the German plan was to defeat France as quickly as possible. Soon all Europe would be at war.

Rivalry

In the early twentieth century there was much rivalry between the great powers in Europe. The Kaiser of Germany hoped to bring Russia into the alliance Germany already had with Austria and Italy, to make sure that France did not get help from Russia in order to strengthen her power against Germany. The Czar of Russia wanted a more general treaty which would include France, and which would be directed mainly against Britain and Japan. All countries said they did not want war, but they all increased the size and strength of their armies and navies. Germany widened the Kiel Canal so that her warships could get easily from the Baltic to the North Sea. In reply Britain built the first Dreadnoughts, the most powerful warships in the world, and made a friendly agreement with Russia. The Kaiser was very angry, and complained that Britain was trying to encircle Germany, but France was pleased, and Britain and France became more friendly. It seemed that the main countries of Europe were dividing into two hostile groups.

Could war be prevented?

In 1912 socialists from several countries met to try to agree on a plan for the working people of all countries to unite in preventing war. They agreed to meet again in August 1914, to work out in detail what they would do. The meeting never took place. Later in 1912 war did break out, but at first it was limited to south-east Europe, where Greece, Bulgaria, Rumania and Serbia were all parts of the Turkish empire. Encouraged by Russia, they joined in war against Turkey, and soon beat her and gained their freedom. This did not please Austria, as some of the Serbs lived in part of the Austrian empire, and a free Serbia would be likely to encourage them to revolt. Ill feeling between Austria and the new Serbia and her Russian backer increased, and Austria prepared for war, knowing that if Russia supported Serbia, Germany would support her. The Russians were building up their army, and the Kaiser thought it might be best to force a war on Russia as soon as possible. This would bring in France, as the ally of Russia. Germany had worked out a plan to destroy the French armies in the first few weeks of a war, and then Germany and Austria could bring all their forces against Russia. Britain was not expected to take part in such a war.

War

In the summer of 1914 the Austrian Archduke, heir to the throne, was shot by a Serbian. This was Austria's opportunity, and she declared war on Serbia. Russia prepared her army to support Serbia. Sir Edward Grey, Britain's Foreign Secretary, suggested that Austrian and Russian leaders should meet to discuss the matter, but they refused. Even the Kaiser was not sure that he wanted war just then, and he urged Austria and Russia to talk things over; but it was too late: the armies were on the move, so on 1 August Germany declared war on Russia. France began to move her troops to support her ally Russia, and on 3 August Germany declared war on France. What was Britain to do?

Many British people thought that it was a struggle between European countries, and no concern of Britain, but others feared that if France was quickly overrun, a stronger Germany might turn on Britain. Few British people knew to what extent Britain had promised to help France if she were attacked, but the French fully expected Britain to come to her help. Then Germany acted in a way which decided British opinion. The frontier between France and Germany was well protected by fortresses, so the German armies decided to march through Belgium, and so get at France across a weakly defended frontier. Germany, France and Britain had all agreed that Belgium would be kept free from war. Britain therefore warned Germany that if she did not agree to withdraw her troops from Belgium, Britain would enter the war against her. There was no reply, so at midnight on 4 August, Britain was at war. The socialist parties in the various countries, who had hoped to prevent a war by the action of workers everywhere, almost all

Men and women filling shells. The risks of explosion were very high. This factory was in Nottingham.

supported their own countries in the war. A few individuals refused to take part in any activity that might help the war effort, and some of them were imprisoned.

In Belgium and France the Germans advanced rapidly, and it looked as though they would capture Paris, but the Russians were also advancing into Germany more quickly than the Germans had expected, and some German troops were transferred from France to meet them in the east. The British 'contemptible little army' as the Kaiser called it, joined with the French and Belgians in a desperate series of defence battles, and Paris was saved. The German plan was foiled. Both sides then dug themselves in, in long lines of trenches, in which for the next three and a half years, millions of men lived and died in mud, dirt and vermin.

A world-wide war

Meanwhile the Japanese entered the war as Britain's ally, and the British, French and Japanese navies rounded up all the German ship-ping, and helped in the conquest of German colonies in various parts of the world. A blockade of the territories of Germany and Austria was maintained, and gradually supplies of food and other vital resources were greatly reduced. In reply German submarines blockaded Britain, sinking at sight ships bringing supplies that were sorely needed.

Italy had signed a treaty of alliance with Germany, but instead of joining the war on Germany's side, she waited until May, 1915, and then joined Britain and France. In the east, after early successes, the Russians were driven back, and in 1917 a revolution led to Russia's withdrawal from the war. To more than balance this loss of an ally, in April, 1917, the USA entered the war. The German submarine attacks on American ships had aroused American anger against Germany.

In 1918 the Austrian empire began to break up, as Czechs, Croats, Serbs and Slovaks set up separate governments. On the western front the Germans were gradually driven back. On 9 November a republic was proclaimed, and the Kaiser fled to Holland. On 11 November the war was over.

Exercises and things to do

Archduke Franz Ferdinand and his wife, killed at Sarajevo.

1 Write out, filling in the blanks. One – stands for each missing letter.

In the early twentieth century there was rivalry between the main countries of – – – – –. They divided into two groups: the – – – – – – Alliance of Germany, – – – – – – – and – – – – –, and an alliance between – – – – – – and – – – – – –, with whom Britain had friendly agreements.

    In 1914 – – – – – – – declared war on – – – – – –, when a Serbian shot the Austrian heir to the throne. – – – – – – prepared to support Serbia, so – – – – – – – declared war on Russia. Then – – – – – – prepared to support – – – – – –, so – – – – – – – declared war on France. To defeat France quickly, the – – – – – – army began to move through – – – – – – –, and this brought – – – – – – – into the war on 4 August – – – –.

    In 1917 the – – – entered the war against – – – – – – –, and in November – – – –, Germany surrendered.

2 The heads and tails of these statements have been mixed. Write them out correctly.

(a) The Kaiser	(1) was the ruler of Russia.
(b) Serbia	(2) was invaded by Germany in 1914.
(c) Russia	(3) entered the war in 1917.
(d) The Czar	(4) complained that Britain was trying to encircle his country.
(e) Belgium	(5) gained her independence from Turkey.
(f) The USA	(6) withdrew from the war in 1917.

3 *Statements of fact* Write out the four statements in each group in what you think is their order of importance or interest. Say in each group why you decided to put one particular statement first.

(a) In the early twentieth century
  (1) there was rivalry between the great powers.
  (2) Germany wanted to prevent France getting help from Russia.
  (3) in most countries all young men had to do military service.
  (4) the main countries of Europe were dividing into two groups.

(b) The First World War
  (1) began in the summer of 1914.
  (2) involved the USA and Japan as well as the main countries in Europe.
  (3) led to the break-up of the Austrian empire.
  (4) left many problems unsolved.

(c) During the First World War
  (1) there was a revolution in Russia.
  (2) each side blockaded the other.
  (3) each side used poison gas and dropped bombs from aircraft.
  (4) millions were killed and wounded in trench warfare.

4 *The right order* Write these out in the order in which they happened.

(a) Revolution in Russia.
(b) Italy joined France and Britain.
(c) A republic was set up in Germany.
(d) Belgium was invaded by Germany.

5 *The main idea* Write out the one sentence which tells what you think is the main idea of this topic.

(a) The Germans failed to win the war.
(b) Britain, France, Russia, Italy and the USA beat Germany and Austria.
(c) Terrible suffering and destruction failed to solve Europe's problems.
(d) Germany became a republic and the Austrian empire was broken up.

Women took on jobs previously done by men. They got good wages but the work was often hard and dangerous. Suffragette activity stopped during the war. The poster also shows a new form of warfare – the aeroplane.

6 Using these characters to represent the countries, draw a comic strip to show the build-up to World War I. Show these episodes: Austria declares war on Serbia, Russia prepares her army to support Serbia, Germany declares war on Russia, France supports Russia, Germany declares war on France, Germany invades Belgium, Britain declares war on Germany.

7 Design a poster calling either for men to join the British Army or women to work in a munitions factory.

8 Complete this chart to show how Europe was divided in the First World War.

Britain's side	Germany's side
Britain	Germany
France	Austria

A 1917 painting by the war artist, John Nash. British soldiers in a trench are surrounded by devastation.

I WANT YOU FOR U.S. ARMY

The Americans entered the war against Germany in 1917.

Lives lost in World War I	
Great Britain	750,000
France	1,500,000
Germany	1,500,000
America	88,000

9 (a) Explain why the USA did not join the war in 1914 but did in 1917.
(b) Explain why Russia withdrew from the war in 1917.

10 Imagine you are either a soldier at the front or a woman war worker. Write a letter describing either your life in the trenches or your work in the factory.

14 Revolution in Russia

In 1900 the Russian empire was the largest single realm in the world. Most of the people were poor peasants, who could neither read nor write, but in St Petersburg, Moscow and one or two other cities there were some very large factories with thousands of workers. The emperor or tsar ruled the country without any sort of parliament. There was much discontent among the factory workers, students, and some of the middle classes because they had no votes, no share in the government. The peasants were discontented because of their terrible poverty.

Bloody Sunday

One Sunday in 1905, when war between Russia and Japan was making life even harder for the workers and peasants, a priest led a great crowd to

A Russian cartoon showing Lenin sweeping away kings, priests and those who were wealthy. The Bolsheviks fought for the control of society by the workers.

ТОВ. Ленин ОЧИЩАЕТ землю от нечисти.

ask humbly that the Czar would make life a little less hard, and that he would set up a sort of parliament. The Czar was not in the palace, but his uncle ordered the troops to fire on the unarmed crowd of men, women and children. Hundreds were killed.

During the next few months there were strikes and riots, and committees of workers and peasants, called soviets, were set up to organize the attempt at revolution. Soon, however, the leaders were either put to death or sent to exile in Siberia. The Czar called a Parliament called the Duma, but it had scarcely any power, and few people had the right to vote for its members.

During the early years of the First World War things in Russia went from bad to worse. Millions of soldiers were killed or taken prisoner. Many of the troops were without rifles, ammunition or boots. Food at home was terribly short, and the shops were empty. On 8 March 1917, the women of Petrograd, as St Petersburg was then called, came together in crowds, calling for bread. Workers from the factories joined them. Then some of the soldiers left their barracks and joined too. The next day there were larger crowds. Some soldiers fired on the people, but more soldiers joined them, arms were seized, the secret police headquarters was sacked and the prisoners released.

Within eight days the first stage of the revolution was over: the Czar abdicated and a provisional government of middle class politicians took control, while at the same time the soviets of workers, soldiers and peasants were formed. The Petrograd soviet took charge of the city's food supply, police and army.

Lenin and the Bolsheviks

Lenin, the leader of the communist revolutionaries known as Bolsheviks, had been exiled, and was living in Zurich. The Germans hoped that he would be able to persuade the Russians to withdraw from the war, so he was allowed to travel through Germany to Russia. Under Lenin's guidance, the Bolsheviks demanded that the war should be ended, and that all power should be handed over to the soviets. They promised the people food, land and peace. In July they tried to seize control of Petrograd, but were foiled by the provisional government under Kerensky, and Lenin fled.

The war was going badly, and the troops were deserting in thousands. As Lenin said, 'The army voted for peace with its legs'. The Bolsheviks, with their demand for peace, became more popular. In October, organized by Trotsky, they took over the city, almost without bloodshed, and Kerensky fled. The Bolsheviks quickly gained control of the rest of the country, although in Moscow only after severe fighting. On 7 November Lenin proclaimed that the provisional government was overthrown, and that the soviets would form a government. A congress of soviets from all over the country put power into the hands of a council of people's commissars, that is, people in charge of some particular part of the government. Most of these were Bolsheviks. Lenin was prime minister, and Trotsky was commissar for foreign affairs.

This November revolution was something quite new. It changed more than the type of government, it changed the whole life of the country. It took power from private people, both landowners and factory owners, and put it in the hands of the state, which, it was claimed, would use the power on behalf of all the working people. When an assembly or parliament was called, there was a majority against the Bolsheviks, so Lenin dissolved it. The Bolsheviks claimed that they were not setting up democracy, but a dictatorship of the Communist Bolshevik Party which would rule on behalf of the working people, and would work towards a system in which workers would be educated, and so capable of deciding for themselves what was best for the country. As soon as they could, the Bolsheviks organized education for all; but first the war must be ended.

The new Bolshevik government set about making peace with Germany, but their army had gone to pieces, and they were almost without arms, so they had to accept very harsh terms. A huge amount of territory, including rich corn land, and iron and coal producing areas had to be handed over to the Germans.

Meanwhile the Bolsheviks were hoping that working people in other countries would also rise against their rulers and employers, stop the war, and unite in a world revolution. There were some Russian generals who were raising armies of 'White Russians' to fight against the Bolsheviks, and they were getting help from other countries. British troops landed at Archangel, American and Japanese troops advanced from Siberia, British and French fleets brought troops to the Black Sea,

Russian workmen prepare to dismantle the statue of the Czar. The Russian Revolution was the end of the Romanov family's rule and the start of many changes in Russian society.

Finns, Poles, Rumanians invaded from the west, and all these armies were converging on Moscow and Petrograd, now called Leningrad.

In areas they regained, the White Russians gave back the land to the old landlords, and as a result, many of the peasants flocked to support the Bolsheviks. The White Russians created a 'white terror' to force the people to support them. In return, the Bolsheviks answered with a 'red terror'. Under the leadership of Trotsky, the Bolshevik armies threw back one invading army after another. Then the Poles, helped by the French, invaded southern Russia, and millions of Russian Ukranians were included in the new Poland. The last of the White Russian generals was defeated late in 1921, and finally the Japanese left Vladivostok. The Bolsheviks could at last get on with the task of rebuilding a whole country. For years no repairs had been carried out in the cities, in the factories, on the roads and railways and in the shipyards. Crops had been destroyed, and drainage and lighting systems were in ruins. No clothes or boots had been made for years. Gradually the revolutionary government firmly established itself, and Russia became the first great communist state.

Exercises and things to do

1 Write out, filling in the blanks. One – stands for each missing letter.

In 1900 Russia was the –––––– country in the world, but most of the people were –––– ––––––––. In 1905 the troops were ordered to –––– upon a peaceful ––––– of peasants and –––––––– who were humbly asking the –––– to make life less ––––, and to set up a –––––––––––. There were then ––––– and ––––––, but the leaders were –––––– or sent to ––––– in Siberia. A Russian –––––––––– called the –––– was set up, but it had little –––––.

During the First ––––– –––, life became much ––––––, and in March 1917, the soldiers joined the ––––––, and –––––––––– broke out. The Czar ––––––––, and a provisional government was formed, while workers, –––––––– and –––––––– formed –––––––– to control the country.

Then in October, the leader of the communists, who were called ––––––––––, took over the government and formed a council of people's ––––––––––.

2 The heads and tails of these statements have been mixed. Write them out correctly.

(a) Lenin	(1) was head of the Russian government in 1900.
(b) The Bolsheviks	(2) opposed the revolution.
(c) The Czar	(3) was leader of the Russian communists.
(d) Trotsky	(4) was head of the 1917 provisional government.
(e) A commissar	(5) was a committee of workers, soldiers and peasants.
(f) Kerensky	(6) organized the take-over of Petrograd.
(g) A soviet	(7) was a man in charge of part of government.
(h) The White Russians	(8) were Russian communists.

Barricades in Moscow during the uprising in December 1905. Lenin called this uprising the 'dress rehearsal' for the revolution of 1917.

3 *Statements of fact* Write out the four statements in each group in what you think is their order of importance or interest. Say in each group why you decided to put one particular statement first.

(a) The first attempt at revolution in Russia
  (1) was in 1905 when discontent was widespread.
  (2) followed the shooting down of the people.
  (3) was organized by soviets of workers and peasants.
  (4) involved strikes and riots but failed when the soviet leaders were arrested.

(b) The revolution of 1917
  (1) began with protesting crowds of women.
  (2) first produced a middle class government.
  (3) succeeded when the soldiers joined the workers in Petrograd.
  (4) succeeded when the Czar abdicated.

(c) The second stage of the revolution
  (1) occurred in October 1917.
  (2) was led by Lenin and Trotsky.
  (3) was led by communists.
  (4) led to a communist government under Lenin and Trotsky.

4 *The right order* Write these out in the order in which they happened.

(a) The Red Army ended the civil war.
(b) The Czar abdicated.
(c) Trotsky organized the seizure of Petrograd.

5 *The main idea* Write out the one sentence which tells what you think is the main idea of this topic.
(a) War and bad government led to revolution in which the communists gained control.
(b) Lenin led the Bolsheviks to victory.
(c) The Czar was forced to abdicate.
(d) Workers, peasants, soldiers, students and the middle classes joined against the Czar.

A demonstration of workers in Petrograd in July 1917, with the slogans 'Down with the war!', 'Down with the capitalist ministers!', 'All power to the Soviets!'

6 On the cartoon shown on the previous page Lenin is shown 'sweeping away' certain groups of Russian society. How could he have achieved this in real life?

7 Explain why the Bolsheviks got so much support from working people in Russia.

8 Which groups of people in Russia did not benefit from the Revolution?

9 The Russians made peace with Germany in 1917. How do you think this affected Germany's efforts to win the war against Britain and France and their allies?

10 (a) Which other countries helped the White Russians?
(b) Why did they do this?

11 Imagine you are Lenin. Make a list of your priorities for Russia at the end of the war with your White Russian opponents.

12 Compile short biographies of Czar Nicholas II, Lenin and Trotsky.

61

15 After the war

Problems

Making a peace treaty after the war presented many problems. President Wilson of the United States wanted to set up a League of Nations which would include all the nations of the world, and enable them to discuss problems, and settle them without going to war. He wanted every nation to be free to have its own independent country and government. Clemenceau of France wanted to keep Germany as weak as possible. Lloyd George of Britain favoured the idea of a League of Nations, but did not want Germany to be so harshly treated with the result that the Germans would be longing for revenge. The League was set up, but Germany and the new communist Russia were not at first members. Wilson and Lloyd George agreed to come to the help of France if Germany should attack her, but when Wilson got back to America, the Congress would not agree. Then Lloyd George said that Britain could not undertake the defence of France by herself, and the whole scheme fell through. The French were very angry.

New nation states were formed from the old Austrian empire and from the western parts of the old Russia. All Germany's colonies were taken from her, and shared out among the allies, to be governed in the interest of the native peoples, on behalf of the League of Nations. The Germans were to hand over their merchant fleet, and much coal, timber and other useful materials. They were also to agree that the war had been all their fault. They were to have only a tiny army and navy, and to pay huge sums of money to the allies. These were known as reparations. Some of this was to be paid in goods and some in gold. The amount of money in a country depended upon the amount of gold, and if this increased more quickly than the amount of goods available, prices went up, so when Britain received reparations in gold, the prices of goods went up, which was bad for Britain's trade. In Germany there was less gold, and prices of goods fell, which was good for trade. When Germany paid in ships, there was no need to build ships in Britain, her shipbuilding firms went bankrupt, and British workers in the shipyards were thrown out of work. Meanwhile, to produce the goods the Germans had to send to the allies, they borrowed large sums of money to build up-to-date factories which provided more work for the German people. However, the bankers and traders of the world soon began to lose confidence in German money. Before the war, twenty German marks had been worth £1. In July, 1921 it needed 279 marks to equal £1. The German government began printing more and more paper money. By November it needed nearly 2000 to equal £1, and by the following August it was 4676. When by the next January it was 115,000, it was clear that German money had become worthless, and practically all the German people's savings had vanished. Germany had to start a new issue of money.

It was agreed that Germany could not pay the huge sums of reparations which had been demanded, but she still had to pay quite large amounts. Meanwhile Britain and France had borrowed large sums from America to wage the war and to pay for vast rebuilding work after it, and interest had to be paid on these debts. They did this with the reparations they obtained from Germany, and the USA then lent the money to Germany so that she could pay the reparations. It took a long time for the world to sort out these money problems. There were troubles in Britain, where receiving reparations had led to increased unemployment.

Inflation was fast in Germany in 1923 and stamps had to be overprinted. This 200 Mark stamp is overprinted as 2,000,000 Marks.

Unemployment

One of the ever present fears of British workers has been that they would be thrown out of work. Until 1911 this had meant no wages, and only very small payments from the poor rates. After that date workers in a few industries received a small amount of unemployment pay from an insurance fund to which employers and workers, while they were in work, paid a small amount each week; but unemployment still meant for nearly all unemployed that they were very poor indeed.

After the First World War most of the people in the world were poor, and could not afford to buy British goods. There was not enough trade to use

SUNDAY · PICTORIAL
SALE MORE THAN DOUBLE THAT OF ANY OTHER SUNDAY PICTURE PAPER

Sunday, May 9th, 1926   Price Two Pence

The Great Strike.   Scenes in London

MOUNTED POLICE, ARMED WITH BATONS, CLEARING THE ROAD AT ELEPHANT & CASTLE

Front page of the 'Sunday Pictorial' on the sixth day of the General Strike.

the scores of ships built during the war. Some shipbuilding yards closed down completely, and in some towns such as Jarrow more than half the people were out of work. Japan had captured much of the cotton trade, and unemployment was widespread in the British cotton manufacturing towns.

By 1921 over 2,000,000 workers in Britain were unemployed, and the wages of those in work were reduced. Wages in the coalmining industry were low, and conditions of work were bad. In 1925 the mine owners claimed that the only way they could sell coal abroad was by reducing wages still further, and increasing hours of work. The miners decided to resist. The whole of the trade union movement was behind them, and the railwaymen and transport workers promised to strike in their support. The government was alarmed, and appointed a commission under Sir Herbert Samuel to inquire into the coal industry, and to make suggestions as to what ought to be done. Meanwhile the government offered money to the industry to keep it going, on the old conditions. The threat of widespread strikes appeared to have saved the miners from a wage cut. The commission did recommend a cut, but not so large as the owners had demanded, and it said there should be no increase in hours. Neither miners nor owners would accept the report, and on 30 April 1926 the miners were locked out.

A general strike

The Trade Union Congress decided to support the miners by calling a general strike. On 4 May there were no trains, no buses, no newspapers. All building operations were stopped, all iron and steel works closed down. Was this the beginning of a revolution? The T U C leaders were certainly not revolutionaries; they merely hoped that the strike would force the government to give in to the miners' demands. Many people sympathized with the miners, but many did not agree with general strikes, and they volunteered to man buses and trains, to help break the strike. Sometimes strikers watched the attempts of volunteers with good humour, sometimes there was violence, buses were overturned and police charged the crowds.

When the T U C leaders found that the government were determined to resist, they tried to arrange a settlement, but without success, so on 12 May they called off the strike. Millions of workers could not understand why their leaders had given in. Most of them returned to work, some to find that they had been sacked, or that their wages had been reduced. The miners complained bitterly that they had been betrayed, and continued their hopeless strike for another six months, until starvation drove them back to work on the owners' terms. The next year the government passed an act making general and sympathetic strikes illegal.

63

Exercises and things to do

1 Write out, filling in the blanks. One – stands for each missing letter.

At the Peace Conference after the war, President –––––– of the –––––– –––––– wanted to set up a –––––– of ––––––––, which would try to settle –––––––– between countries without going to war. The French leader, –––––––––– wanted to stop –––––––– from becoming ––––––. The British leader, ––––– –––––– wanted a –––––– of ––––––, but did not want to upset ––––––, so that she would think only of ––––––.

The –––––––– empire, and parts of ––––––– were made into new –––––– states. –––––––– was told she must pay the whole –––– of the war. These payments were called ––––––––––––. To help Germany to pay these, –––––––– lent her large sums of money.

2 The heads and tails of these statements have been mixed. Write them out correctly.

(a) Reparations	(1) were colonies taken from Germany and ruled by other countries on behalf of the League of Nations.
(b) Clemenceau	(2) was president of America.
(c) Sir Herbert Samuel	(3) was president of France.
(d) Wilson	(4) put the British point of view at the Peace Conference.
(e) Mandates	(5) were payments to pay the costs of the war.
(f) Lloyd George	(6) headed the commission on the coal industry.

3 *Statements of fact* Write out the four statements in each group in what you think is their order of importance or interest. Say in each group why you decided to put one particular statement first.

(a) After the First World War the Peace Conference
  (1) set up a League of Nations.
  (2) blamed Germany for the war.
  (3) divided most of the Austrian empire into separate nation states.
  (4) demanded large reparations from Germany.

(b) The payment of reparations
  (1) caused difficulties for those who had to pay them and for those who received them.
  (2) led to Germany borrowing large sums of money.
  (3) led to unemployment and high prices in Britain.
  (4) had to be much reduced.

(c) In Britain after the war
  (1) coal miners went on strike when asked to accept even lower wages.
  (2) the Trade Union Congress supported the miners and called a general strike.
  (3) the government refused to provide money for the mining industry.
  (4) the general strike failed, and an act of parliament made general strikes illegal.

4 *The right order* Write these out in the order in which they happened.

(a) The value of money in Germany collapsed.
(b) Receiving reparations in Britain led to unemployment.
(c) A League of Nations was set up.
(d) Germany began to pay reparations.

5 *The main idea* Write out the one sentence which tells what you think is the main idea of this topic.

(a) The peace treaty after the war led to many difficulties.
(b) The payment of reparations by Germany caused unemployment in Britain.
(c) There were disagreements among the winning nations.
(d) The war upset trade and led to low wages and money problems.

The government recruited volunteers to maintain essential supplies and services. Students drove trains and buses, and 'special' constables assisted the police.

THE TIN HAT "SPECIALS".

SIXTH DAY OF THE GREAT STRIKE

No Formal Move by Either Side Towards Negotiations: Government's Firm Stand.

"Call Off" MUST PRECEDE PARLEYS

Volunteer Transport And Other Services Improving Rapidly Everwhere

BY OUR POLITICAL CORRESPONDENT.

The fifth day of the General Strike has passed without any change in the main position. There has been no formal move towards any resumption of negotiations between the Government and the Trades Union Congress General Council.

The Prime Minister's declaration still stands that the General Strike order must be withdrawn before there can be any discussion of peace. To this, so far, the answer of the T.U.C. has been an uncompromising "no."

The Cabinet declares firmly that it will not and cannot proceed to discuss terms while any question of intimidation remains.

Nevertheless, there have been certain reported tentative moves—apparently confined to Labour men in the House of Commons—to find some formula on which they could base steps to make a new approach to the Government.

Sooner or later I feel there will be overtures from the T.U.C., but in the present condition of feeling on both sides I feel also no period can yet be prophesied as the limit of the crisis.

Meanwhile, services of every kind are improving steadily, and everywhere all possible normal activities of life are being maintained.

It was stated in the best-informed circles yesterday that the Government will take an early opportunity of passing legislation to free labour from the conditions enforced upon it by the exercise of the existing trades union laws.

:AX NOT YET.

als Needed in London
' To-morrow.

issued by the Government

disorder has occurred in any
intry.
ss, as was to be expected,
. becoming more intense and
ot yet reached.
sed to raise the numbers of
oles in London as quickly as
)00.
, Sir William Joynson-Hicks
he 50,000 specials—another
ndon by to-morrow.

EWS ITEMS

orecast; showery, with

LONDON'S TRAFFIC NEARLY NORMAL.

Splendid Volunteers on Tubes and Buses.

80,000 MEN FOR SERVICE.

London has solved the bulk of its traffic transport problems.

Yesterday saw an easing of the trouble of getting to work, for many business houses decided to count the half day out altogether. There were consequently fewer workers, fewer seekers for "lifts" from the volunteer motor-car transport, and a general lessening of the demands on tubes and underground railways.

It is, however, the fact that on most of the latter lines the position reached on Friday evening was that of service not far removed from normal. On "the Met" there will even be an increase of Sunday Services.

The volunteers who have taken on the task of keeping London's railways going have been splendid. Many are possessed of considerable technical skill.

"PROUD OF YOU."

Lord Ashfield, Chairman of the Underground Railways, in a message thanking those who are helping to re-establish "Services" says: "We are proud of you"

The tube train driver in gloves and pullover quite obviously knows his job, as do his fellows the guard and amateur lift man

Omnibus services organised by the London General Company have steadily increased and yesterday several hundreds were available, many of them running almost normal services at few minute intervals.

To date some 80,000 volunteers have been enrolled in London.

The Main Line Railways have now reached services averaging more than 700 trains per day and are increasing their services daily. There will be no passenger trains from Euston to-day.

SOVIET MONEY GIFT

Moscow, Saturday

The General Council of the Trades Union of Soviet Republics has transferred

A page from the 'Sunday Pictorial'.

> 'In the street we saw convoys of food supplies under the protection of soldiers and armoured cars. Hyde Park was a food depot and the public was kept out. Newspapers shrank to one page leaflets and those of us who had wireless sets invited others to listen to the news. We used our car to take people to and from their work. The few omnibuses which ran had boarded up windows and engines protected by barbed wire.'
>
> C. S. Peel, *Life's Enchanted Cup* (1933)

6 Explain what you can see on the cartoon shown on this page.

7 Make a list of some of the events which you think led up to the General Strike.

8 Draw two posters – one calling for support for the General Strike and one opposing it.

9 Write an article for a newsheet (there were no newspapers) describing something that happened during the General Strike.

10 How were convoys and buses protected? Why were they protected?

11 How did people find out about the General Strike?

12 Make a list of the results of the General Strike.

UNDER WHICH FLAG?

JOHN BULL. "ONE OF THESE TWO FLAGS HAS GOT TO COME DOWN—AND IT WON'T BE MINE."

'Punch's' version of the General Strike

16 World depression

World dependence

Most countries of the world depend upon others for their prosperity, through trade, and the lending of money to help trade and industry. After the First World War the United States of America was very prosperous, and lent large sums to Germany, Austria and other countries so that they could obtain large quantities of goods from America, and pay for them very gradually over a long period of years.

The stock market

American industries were making big profits, and people rushed to buy shares in them, and so get some of the profits. Share prices on the New York stock market doubled and doubled again. Then in October 1929 people began to doubt whether the shares were really worth such high prices, and they began to sell them before prices fell. Soon everybody else was trying to sell too, and prices fell rapidly. People who had borrowed money in order to buy shares at high prices now sold them at low prices rather than risk losing them altogether, so they were unable to repay the money they had borrowed from the banks, and many of these had

to close down. Thousands of people were ruined. People stopped buying goods and factories closed down, employees were thrown out of work and wages were reduced. Soon millions of unemployed were tramping the streets, begging. There were plenty of raw materials waiting to be manufactured, plenty of well-equipped factories to use them, plenty of men waiting for work – but nobody had the confidence to use the factories to employ the men to work up the raw materials into things people needed. So the richest country in the world was swept by poverty and want.

The depression spreads

In the modern world, depression cannot be limited to one country. The Americans ceased buying from other countries, and instead of lending to them, wanted their money back. European factories and banks closed down, and unemployment increased. But the depression did not stop there. Europeans could no longer afford to buy so much food and raw materials from countries such as Australia and Argentina, and there too, there was unemployment with growing distress. Wheat which could not be sold was ploughed in; coffee was burned or dumped into the sea, fields were left

The collapse of the American stock market in October 1929 was the beginning of a world economic depression. Here mounted police control crowds outside the stock exchange on Wall Street, New York.

unplanted; yet in other parts of the world people were starving, and in other places there were empty, idle ships that could have carried the food to where it was needed; and everywhere there were millions of unemployed workers. Countries which a few years previously had produced thousands of millions of pounds to make guns and explosives in the war, could not now produce the few hundreds of millions that could have restored employment and trade. In Britain there were 3,000,000 unemployed, in Germany 6,000,000, in the USA nearly 15,000,000.

How to beat the depression
In Britain the Labour government thought they must save money, and that they could not afford to pay out so much government money, and suggested that unemployment pay should be reduced. Most of the government ministers would not agree, so Ramsay MacDonald, the prime minister, joined with the Conservatives and Liberals to form a National Government, but they did not know what to do for the best. While the British government cut down their spending, some economists argued that they ought to spend more, to provide work and increase confidence.

The American answer to the depression
The American people were bewildered by the sudden depression. In 1932 the new president, Franklin D. Roosevelt, promised a new deal for the American people. Instead of spending less than before, as the government did in Britain, he called upon the American government to spend more, in order to give the unemployed useful work. Wherever possible, money was used to increase the future wealth of the country, by carrying out schemes of land drainage, afforestation and power production. The biggest scheme was that of the Tennessee Valley Authority.

The Tennessee Valley Act
In 1933 the Tennessee Valley Authority was set up. It had representatives from the main Federal government, the state governments and private contractors. Thirty-two great dams were built to control the water, and to generate electricity, so that if torrential rain turns a particular tributary into a raging torrent, messages are flashed from dam to dam, releasing water from one lake to make room for the flooding water, or holding back water from another, to equalize the flow. Twenty thousand million kilowatt hours of electricity can be produced. In 1933 only three farms out of every

Germany's answer to the depression
'Guns will make us powerful; butter will only make us fat.' said Hermann Goering, Hitler's War Minister. This montage shows a German family eating iron and steel. Hitler (in the picture) was determined to make Germany powerful once again. The jobs created by making weapons also ended unemployment.

hundred had any electricity; now almost all have it, to carry out numerous farm processes. Cheap electricity also made possible the creation of many new industries. The dams have made the river into a long series of lakes, connected by canals, so that the whole 1000 kilometres of the valley are navigable. Within twenty years, fleets of steel barges were carrying 20 times as much freight as in 1933.

In the lakes millions of fish are bred for food. By raising and lowering the level of the lakes, the malaria mosquitoes are killed. The shores of the lakes are laid out as parks, with facilities for swimming and boating. New forests were planted on the slopes to hold the soil together. Tens of thousands of privately owned demonstration farms have been set up, and the people are encouraged to copy the scientific methods. As a result of the working of the TVA, 3,000,000 people in the area were lifted from poverty to reasonable prosperity.

Meanwhile, in the rest of the world, the depression slowly cleared. In the late 1930s fears of another world war encouraged governments to find vast sums of money to make armaments, and many of the unemployed found work.

Exercises and things to do

1 Write out, filling in the blanks. One – stands for each missing letter.

After the First World War the USA was very – – – – – – – – –, and was able to – – – – money to several countries in – – – – – –, to help them to – – – – – and buy many goods from – – – – – – –. Then there was a panic on the – – –   – – – – stock – – – – – –. Banks and – – – – – – – – closed down and millions were thrown – – – of – – – –. This – – – – – – – – – – spread to almost the whole – – – – –. In Britain the government said they must spend – – – – money, so they – – – wages and – – – – – – – – – – – pay. The depression grew – – – – –.

   In America President – – – – – – – – offered the people a – – –   – – – –, and his government spent vast sums of money on schemes which would – – – – – – – – the country's – – – – – – in the future, and at the same time provide – – – – for the – – – – – – – – – –. One big scheme brought prosperity to the people of the – – – – – – – – Valley.

An American farming family during the depression. Many left the land. Roosevelt's 'New Deal' was an effort to overcome depression.

2 The heads and tails of these statements have been mixed. Write them out correctly.

(a) In 1933	(1) the depression started.
(b) The Labour government	(2) tried to cure the depression by spending much more.
(c) Roosevelt	(3) was Prime Minister of Britain.
(d) In 1929	(4) the Tennessee Valley Authority began.
(e) The USA government	(5) thought the way to cure the depression was by cutting government spending.
(f) MacDonald	(6) was head of the USA government.

3 *Statements of fact* Write out the four statements in each group, in what you think is their order of importance or interest. Say in each group why you decided to put one particular statement first.

(a) In the USA after the First World War
   (1) at first there was great prosperity.
   (2) big loans were made to Europe.
   (3) later people lost confidence and were all trying to sell their shares on the stock market.
   (4) many businesses failed and loans to Europe stopped.

(b) The depression in the 1930s
   (1) spread to Europe.
   (2) caused much unemployment in Britain and Germany.
   (3) spread to countries producing food and raw materials.
   (4) became almost world wide.

(c) President Roosevelt
   (1) promised a new deal for the American people.
   (2) took measures in 1932 to beat the depression.
   (3) set up the Tennessee Valley Authority.
   (4) brought prosperity to 3,000,000 people by reorganizing land use and river control.

Watched by crowds of well-wishers, unemployed men of Jarrow march 300 miles to London in 1936 to plead for Government help. They received none.

4 *The right order* Write these out in the order in which they happened.

(a) There was depression in Europe.
(b) Prices fell rapidly on the New York stock exchange.
(c) The depression spread to Australia.
(d) There was great prosperity in the USA.

5 *The main idea* Write out the one sentence which tells what you think is the main idea of this topic.

(a) There were very different ideas on how to combat depression.
(b) The depression in America spread first to Europe, then to most of the rest of the world.
(c) Unemployment in Europe led to depression in food-producing countries.
(d) The effects of the TVA prove the value of large-scale scientific planning.

6 What was the Jarrow Crusade?

7 Look again at the picture on page 67. What clues has the artist used to show that this family in 1936 is German?

8 Complete this grid for Britain, the USA and Germany:

How to beat the depression	
Country	Measures taken
Britain	*Cut spending*

9 Using other books find out the meaning of these phrases: on the dole, the means test, the Labour Exchange, the pawn shop.

17 The Second World War

Above: German soldiers march past the Führer (Adolf Hitler) in Nuremburg in 1936. Hitler promised that Germany would be strong again. After he had been installed legally as Chancellor, he set about re-arming Germany. Part of his plan was the conquest of Europe, including Russia. The Second World War, however, led to his death and the devastation of Germany. In the picture to the left the Russian flag flies over a blazing Berlin. Nazi Germany was destroyed.

The two main causes of the Second World War were the settlement after the First World War, and the discontent caused by the Great Depression. The treatment of Germany at the peace treaty which ended the First World War left its people bitterly angry, and gave German leaders a good reason for trying to get their revenge. The unemployed were easily persuaded to support a leader who promised a better future. Adolf Hitler told the Germans that they were a master race. He formed the Nazi Party which became a sort of private army. At first Hitler got little support, but when the depression caused such hardship in Germany, he was able to recruit large numbers of followers. In 1933 he became chancellor of Germany, and in 1934, president. He began to build up a powerful army, airforce and navy.

Mussolini in Italy

The Italians had changed sides, and come into the First World War on the side of the allies, hoping to gain territory in Europe and Africa from the Austrians and Germans, but in the peace treaty all the Italians got was some small pieces of Austria, and nothing at all in Africa. Many of the ex-service men were disappointed: they wanted to make Italy powerful, and joined a union formed by Mussolini, called the Fascists. They despised Parliament and the socialists, and believed they needed a dictator. They dressed in black shirts, and in 1922, seized the local government offices in many districts. The king asked Mussolini to become prime minister and to form a government.

Mussolini said that peace made people soft – they must be ready to sacrifice themselves for the state, and obey their leader. He demanded more living space for Italy, and looked for easy victims. In 1934 he picked a quarrel with Abyssinia, and invaded the country. The League of Nations, of which both were members, agreed that Italy was in the wrong, but could not agree on what to do about it, since other members of the League did not want to risk war with Italy. So Abyssinia became part of an Italian empire. Hitler supported Mussolini, and the two dictators agreed to work together, and formed a pact called the Rome-Berlin Axis.

Japan

In the Far East Japan was growing desperate. Her population was increasing rapidly, and Japanese workers were not allowed to enter Canada, America and Australia, so they looked anxiously for somewhere else to go. They thought northern China and Manchuria had room for millions of Japanese. The murder of a Japanese officer was used as an excuse for the invasion of northern China. The Chinese appealed to the League of Nations, for both China and Japan were members. The League called upon its members to take action against Japan, but none of them was willing to risk war. The Japanese withdrew from the League, and nothing was done as Japan took over large areas of China. The League seemed quite helpless against any powerful nation that broke the peace.

Hitler

In 1936 Hitler began his action to increase Germany's power and territory. He marched his troops into the Rhineland, from which German forts and troops had been barred by the treaty of 1919. In 1938 he took over Austria and included it in Germany. Later in 1938 he demanded that Czechoslovakia should hand over the north-western part of their country, where many Germans were living, and also break off the Czech alliance with France and Russia. The Czechs refused, and it seemed that Europe was on the verge of war. British, French and Italian leaders had meetings with Hitler, and agreed that the Czechs must give in to Hitler's demands. The following spring Hitler overran the rest of Czechoslovakia, while Italy attacked Albania. At last it became clear to Britain and France that the more they gave in to the dictators, the more they would take, so promises were made to Poland, Greece and Rumania that if they were attacked, Britain and France would help them. Hitler complained that Britain and France were trying to encircle Germany. He said that he was the great defender of western Europe from the danger of communist aggression by Bolshevik Russia, and demanded that Poland should hand over part of her territory to Germany.

On 23 August 1939, the world heard that Germany and Russia, who had appeared to be bitter enemies, had signed a pact not to attack one another. A week later Hitler invaded Poland. On 3 September Britain declared war on Germany. The Second World War had begun.

The war

The German army quickly overran western Poland; while Russian armies took eastern Poland which had many Russian inhabitants in areas which had been seized by Poland in 1921. There was nothing Britain and France could do to help Poland. In the spring of 1940 German armies overran Denmark, Norway, Holland and Belgium, and advanced into France. The French armies collapsed, and the British troops escaped back to Britain through Dunkirk. Britain was left alone to face the might of Germany.

The Battle of Britain began with massive air attacks. Mussolini entered the war, and said he was proud to play his part in bombing London. The British air force was so effective that German hopes of invading Britain faded. In June 1941 Hitler invaded Russia, and at first advanced far into the country, but the Russians fought back and held Leningrad and Moscow.

The war spreads

Meanwhile the Japanese thought they saw their chance to drive the British, French, Dutch and Americans from the Far East. In December 1941 Japanese aircraft attacked the American fleet in Pearl Harbour without warning. Britain declared war on Japan, and Germany and Italy declared war on America.

At first the Japanese were successful everywhere, but then everywhere the tide turned. In the summer of 1942 America won two great naval victories; in October the British army in north Africa won the battle of El Alamein against the Germans, and in November the Russians began a great offensive at Stalingrad. Throughout 1943 the Japanese, Germans and Italians were slowly driven back. In June 1944 British and American armies invaded France, and by August Paris was freed. The Germans fought desperately. Flying bombs and rocket bombs were directed at London and other British cities, but their launching sites were captured as the allied armies advanced. In 1945 Russian troops were invading Germany from the east, and British and Americans from the west. In May Hitler's death was announced, Berlin surrendered, and the war in the west was ended.

The war against Japan continued until August, when two atom bombs were dropped on Japanese cities. The destruction and death rate were terrible, and Japan surrendered.

Exercises and things to do

1 Write out, filling in the blanks. One – stands for each missing letter.

The German people were very ––––– at the way ––––––– had been treated in the ––––– treaty in 1919, and many wanted their –––––––, so they were ready to support ––––– ––––––– when he said he would make Germany great again.

The Italians also were ––––––––––– with the peace treaty, so they supported ––––––––– who joined with –––––– to form the –––– - ––––––– Axis. In 1938 the Germans took over ––––––– and part of –––––––––––––. In 1939 –––––– invaded ––––––. Britain and –––––– had promised to help –––––– and they declared war on Germany. Soon almost all –––––– was involved in the war. In 1941 Germany attacked ––––––, and ––––– attacked the U S A.

2 The heads and tails of these statements have been mixed. Write them out correctly.

(a) Mussolini	(1) took over Czechoslovakia.
(b) Abyssinia	(2) was attacked by Japan.
(c) The Japanese	(3) shared Poland with Hitler.
(d) Hitler	(4) became dictator of Italy.
(e) Manchuria	(5) was invaded by Italy.
(f) The Russians	(6) attacked the U S A at Pearl Harbour.

A German cartoon showing the Japanese invasion of Manchuria in 1932. In (1) the Japanese invade. In (2) they commit atrocities. (3) shows the League of Nations sending a note to Japan and (4) shows Japan victorious, having ignored the note.

3 *Statements of fact* Write out the four statements in each group in what you think is their order of importance or interest. Say in each group why you decided to put one particular statement first.

(a) The war was caused because
  (1) Hitler attacked Poland.
  (2) the Germans were angry at the terms of the 1919 peace treaty.
  (3) Hitler wanted to make Germany great again.
  (4) Britain and France feared that the dictators would go on swallowing up other countries.

(b) The Japanese
  (1) wanted more land for their growing population.
  (2) invaded northern China.
  (3) attacked the American fleet at Pearl Harbour.
  (4) surrendered after two atomic bombs had been dropped on their cities.

4 *The right order* Write these out in the order in which they happened.

(a) Atom bombs were dropped on Japan.
(b) Mussolini invaded Abyssinia.
(c) Hitler invaded Russia.
(d) Japan attacked Pearl Harbour.

5 *The main idea* Write out the one sentence which tells what you think is the main idea of this topic.

(a) The Second World War lasted from 1939 to 1945.
(b) Many people in Germany, Italy and Japan believed they could cure their discontents by war.
(c) Hitler thought the Germans were a master race and could conquer the rest of the world.
(d) Britain, France and America were determined to prevent the dictators overrunning the smaller countries.

WILLS'S CIGARETTES

THE CIVILIAN RESPIRATOR—HOW TO ADJUST IT

THE CIVILIAN RESPIRATOR—HOW TO ADJUST IT. Great care must be taken to see that the respirator is correctly fitted and adjusted, in order that a supply of pure air, quite free from gas, is ensured for breathing. The respirator is made so that it fits closely round the face, and is provided with adjustable straps to hold it in the correct position. It is important that the respirator be tried on and the straps properly adjusted to the requirements of the wearer (see picture), so that it may be put on at a moment's notice. (See also Cards Nos. 27 and 29). (No. 28)

THE CIVILIAN RESPIRATOR—HOW TO REMOVE IT. The picture shows the RIGHT way to take off a Civilian Respirator. This should be done by slipping the head harness forward from the back of the head. It is important that the respirator should be taken off in this way. The WRONG way to take it off is by taking hold of the metal box containing the filters and pulling the face-piece off the chin. By this method there is a danger of bending and cracking the transparent window. If this window is cracked, the respirator is useless. (No. 29)

A.R.P

Britain feared that Germany would use gas as a weapon against civilians. Everyone was issued with a gas mask and had to carry it with them at all times.

War artist Laura Knight shows women hauling down barrage balloons around the bombed industrial city of Coventry. Barrage balloons were floated above cities to prevent enemy aircraft from flying too low.

6 Look closely at the picture of the Nuremburg march on page 70. Describe the scene, picking out details from the photograph.

7 Make a list of the reasons why people would support Mussolini.

8 Copy out the map of Europe and label each country. Now shade in those countries which were invaded by Germany.

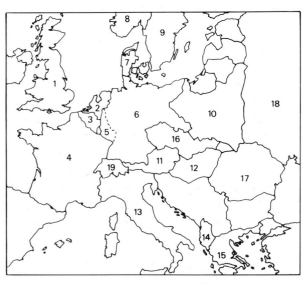

1 Britain, 2 Holland, 3 Belgium, 4 France, 5 Rhineland, 6 Germany, 7 Denmark, 8 Norway, 9 Sweden, 10 Poland, 11 Austria, 12 Hungary, 13 Italy, 14 Albania, 15 Greece, 16 Czechoslovakia, 17 Rumania, 18 Russia, 19 Switzerland.

9 As a war correspondent for the *Daily News* send back your report describing either the Russian entry into Berlin or the destruction of Hiroshima.

10 Complete this grid using the information given in this chapter.

World War II 1939–45	
Year	**Major event(s)**
1939	*Germany invades Poland*
1939	*Britain and France declare war on Germany*

The Japanese city of Hiroshima was destroyed when the Americans dropped the first atomic bomb.

18 Communism and socialism

Communism and socialism are sets of ideas about how people should live, and how the government of a country should be organized. Like many ideas, they are difficult to put into practice, and some people who begin trying to carry them out become so affected by the difficulties they meet, or by the power they gain, that they produce a state of affairs quite different from that which they intended to bring about. Although Christ taught people to love and serve one another, Christians killed other Christians in the cruellest way in the name of the Christian religion. So it has been with communism. The first Christians were in a way, communists – that is, they had everything in common. All who joined them sold all their possessions, and the money obtained was put into a common fund. All had simple food, clothing and shelter, and the rest was used to help people who were in need.

Karl Marx

Modern communism was explained by Karl Marx in 1848, in the Communist Manifesto. He maintained that the ruling class and the employers take nearly all the wealth for themselves, and give the working class by way of wages, as little as they possibly can. Marx thought the life of the workers would continually get worse; but then, he said, would come the revolution, when the workers would seize control of the factories and the government for themselves. He thought that most of the workers would not at first understand the situation properly, so their leaders would form a 'dictatorship of the proletariat', that is, the leaders who were members of the Communist Party would govern the country in what they considered were the interests of the working class. This is what happened in Russia. The idea was that in time, when the workers had been educated, there would no longer be any classes, no rich and poor, but that all would be able equally to take part in running the country and its industries. This is what socialists hope to bring about, but unlike the communists they do not think this can only be brought about by revolution, but that it can be done gradually, by peaceful methods.

Nobody in a communist state would be allowed to own factories, banks, railways, mines, etc., to make profits from them. All these things would be run by the state for the benefit of all. 'From each according to his ability, to each according to his needs' was the motto. When communists have

A George Cruickshank cartoon showing poor dressmakers climbing stairs and falling into a 'profit making' machine which produces cheap dresses and money. The machine is driven by a capitalist. Those who benefit are the shopkeepers, the people who can afford to buy the clothes, and the capitalist.

gained power, they have set up what are known as totalitarian states, that is, they allowed no other party but the Communist Party to exist, and their secret police have claimed the right to interfere with the freedom of the people, to ensure the safety of the state. This has given some leaders of Communist Parties the power to kill any people who, they fear, might be threatening their power, as Stalin did in Russia. Writers, artists and scientists were not allowed to write, speak or act freely, but had to take orders from the party leaders. Children, on the other hand, are well looked after in most communist countries: they have first claim on milk and other important foods. Millions of Russian children who never had any chance of going to school under the old system were given education, and many adults too were taught to read and write.

Many communists believe that it is their duty to spread communism to other countries, and they try to stir up discontent and revolution wherever they can. The governments of capitalist, non-communist countries therefore feel that communism is a threat to their existence.

The beginnings of socialism in Britain

During the Second World War the state had been obliged to control much of the life of the British people. Men and women were conscripted for the forces, or for war work or the coal mines. Employers had to produce things the government wanted, and trade unionists had to go to work where they were needed. Strikes by workers and lock-outs by employers were forbidden. Food and clothing were rationed, and prices were controlled. The health of the poorer section of the nation actually improved during the war, and unemployment and destitution were abolished.

When the war ended in 1945, this 'wartime socialism' seemed to many people to be better than the 'free for all' of the years before the war. In the General Election of 1945 the Labour Party, which had a programme which aimed at an increase in socialism, gained a big majority. The Labour government began to transform war socialism into what they hoped would be true socialism – not the communism of Russia, which seemed to have destroyed the freedom to think and speak and write in opposition to the government, but a British form of democratic socialism, which gave fair shares to all, but left all free in thought and personal matters. The Labour government hoped to avoid unemployment, and to introduce a scheme of social security which would protect all citizens from hardship through

Lloyd-George's 'Right Ticket'.
David Lloyd George paved the way for the Welfare State in his reforms of 1909–1911. National Insurance, paid for by workers, employers and the state, provided some social security for those in need.

bad health, old age and other personal misfortunes. The good things of life were to be shared more fairly among all people. Banking, coal, gas, electricity, public transport and iron and steel were to be taken from private ownership and nationalized.

Most of Britain's export trade had vanished during the war, and the government did everything possible to revive it, and to repair the widespread damage to houses and factories. For a time it was possible to buy food and raw materials from abroad only by borrowing large sums from the USA and Canada. All the best clothing, furniture, pottery, cars and other things had to be reserved for export, and the people in Britain had to continue going without, and to put up with rationing. In spite of the difficulties, in 1947 the National Health Service was introduced, which gave every man, woman and child the right to free medical attendance, medicine, hospital treatment, spectacles and dental treatment. Pensions, unemployment and sickness pay were improved. And so, building on the work begun during the war, the Labour government constructed the 'Welfare State' which looked after everyone 'from the cradle to the grave'. When later the Conservatives formed the government, apart from repealing the nationalization of road transport and part of the iron and steel industry, they retained the socialist measures of the Labour government. It appeared that the Welfare State had come to stay, and Britain remained a mixed economy, that is, some industries and services were run by the state, but many kinds of production and business were in the hands of private owners and employers.

Exercises and things to do

1 Write out, filling in the blanks. One – stands for each missing letter.

Communism and socialism are ways of ————————— a country, of ————————— industry and of sharing out —————— among the people. Both aim at giving to all the —————— control over these things, but while most ————————— believe that the change from capitalism can be obtained gradually and peaceably through acts of —————————, most ————————— believe that it can be done only by ————————— and the use of force.

Where communists have formed a government, the —————— have tended to keep the power in their own hands, and have not allowed any —————— political ———————, thus forming a ————————— state, with —————— police to stop any opposition.

Democratic ————————— aims at forming a ——————— state where ——— the people are protected against sickness, old age and —————————, etc., and where —————— is shared out more fairly. The —————— controls the most important services and —————————, but leaves people ———— to think for themselves, and to form other ————————— parties.

Chinese workers being educated at the school in Niutung People's commune. Note the picture of Mao Tse-Tung.

2 The heads and tails of these statements have been mixed. Write them out correctly.

(a) A mixed economy (1) is a system where as much as possible is left to free private enterprise.

(b) Capitalism (2) is a type of state where some services and industries are run by the state, and others by individual owners and employers.

(c) Karl Marx (3) was a Russian leader who killed those who threatened his power.

(d) Totalitarian states (4) are countries where all the people can vote freely for whichever party they wish.

(e) Stalin (5) wrote the Communist Manifesto.

(f) Democratic states (6) are countries which have only one political party.

3 *Statements of fact* Write out the four statements in each group in what you think is their order of importance or interest. Say in each group why you decided to put one particular statement first.

(a) Communism
  (1) does not believe in large-scale ownership of private property and industry.
  (2) was practised by the early Christians.
  (3) was explained by Karl Marx.
  (4) is regarded by capitalists as a threat to their existence.

(b) Karl Marx
  (1) described his theory of communism in 1848.
  (2) believed that class war would lead to communism.
  (3) thought that under capitalism the life of the working class would grow worse.
  (4) believed that the only way to a fair system for the workers was through revolution.

(c) During the Second World War
  (1) men and women were conscripted for work or the forces.
  (2) strikes and lock-outs were forbidden.
  (3) prices were controlled and goods were rationed.
  (4) the government controlled much of the life of the people.

A photograph of young people dancing taken by Henri Cartier-Bresson in 1952.

4 *The right order* Write these out in the order in which they happened.

(a) Karl Marx explained communism.
(b) A national health service was introduced into Britain.
(c) The early Christians held everything in common.
(d) The dictatorship of the proletariat was set up in Russia.

5 *The main idea* Write out the one sentence which tells what you think is the main idea of this topic.

(a) Communism is a kind of socialism.
(b) War made a kind of socialism necessary in Britain.
(c) War conditions and Labour governments put some socialist ideas into practice, and the Conservatives retained most of them.
(d) The idea behind communism is fair and equal sharing, but communist states tend to be dictatorships.

6 Describe what you can see in the Cruickshank cartoon on page 74.

7 (a) List four of the benefits of 'buying' Lloyd George's 'Right Ticket'.
 (b) Who do you think might oppose the scheme and why?

8 Look at the photograph above taken by Cartier-Bresson. In which country do you think it was taken? Give reasons, if you can, for your answer.

9 Describe what you can see in the picture of the Chinese commune opposite. Are there any similarities with the Cartier-Bresson picture on this page?

10 (a) In what ways did the government in Britain have control over people's lives during the Second World War?
 (b) What difficulties did the Labour Government face at the end of the war?
 (c) What is the Welfare State?

11 Why do you think communist and democratic countries oppose each other?

19 After the war: the USA and Russia

At the end of the Second World War Germany was divided by the victors into occupied zones, Britain, with the rest of Europe was exhausted, Japan was utterly defeated and Russia had suffered terrible losses of life and damage to industry and homes. The USA, on the other hand, had suffered no damage at home, and had built up a vast productive power. The Americans had overwhelming naval superiority over the rest of the world, and she alone possessed the secret of the making of the atomic bomb. Two main problems faced the USA: the danger of a trade depression, and the fear of the spread of communism. The end of the demand for huge quantities of war materials threatened her industry with depression and her people with unemployment. At the same time the confused state of Europe after the war might encourage communism there. To counter both these threats, the United States government created the Marshall Plan. This offered to help the countries of Europe to combine in ways of recovering from the terrible destruction due to the war, and offered to provide large sums of money, so that they could buy vast quantities of goods which American industry could produce.

At home, the standard of living in the USA was boosted by producing more and bigger cars, refrigerators, washing machines, processed foods and many other things which people were persuaded to buy through high-pressure advertising. Vast sums of money were spent on armaments to counter the growing strength of Russia.

Russia

After the revolution in 1917, the Russian communist government had to fight for its existence against French, British, Japanese, German, Finnish and Polish invading armies. In the Second World War about 25,000,000 Russians, soldiers and civilians, were killed, 1,280,000 square kilometres of Russian land – ten times the total area of England – were devastated, 64,000 kilometres of railroad tracks were torn up, 1700 towns and 70,000 villages were razed to the ground, 30,000 factories were destroyed, and countless tractors, locomotives and wagons; and all this destruction was done by Germany, a country which had signed a treaty of non-aggression with Russia only two years before. The Russians had therefore good reason to be suspicious of all capitalist countries. When the USA, under the Marshall Plan, offered aid to all countries of Europe, Russia refused to take part, believing that the American capitalists were trying to gain control of much of European industry. Russia prevented the eastern European countries which were under her control from taking part in the plan also. To counter this, and to help the communist countries to work together, and to strengthen Russia against the capitalist world, the Russians set up the Cominform; and so Russia brought down what Mr Winston Churchill called the 'iron curtain' between the communist and capitalist worlds. The 'cold war' set in in earnest. In 1949 Russia made a treaty with China, where the communists under Mao Tse-Tung had gained control. The communist world was growing.

Meanwhile Russia was making wonderful progress in science and industry. Even during the war

The USA was the strongest and richest country at the end of World War II. Americans had a much better standard of living than the rest of the world.

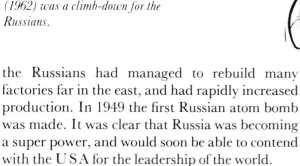

By the 1960s the Russians had developed their own nuclear weapons and could challenge the USA. Here Nikita Khruschev (USSR) and President Kennedy (USA) engage in a trial of strength. The Cuban Missile Crisis (1962) was a climb-down for the Russians.

the Russians had managed to rebuild many factories far in the east, and had rapidly increased production. In 1949 the first Russian atom bomb was made. It was clear that Russia was becoming a super power, and would soon be able to contend with the USA for the leadership of the world.

Although the Americans had quickly disbanded most of their troops after the war, they still continued to spend a great deal of money on military preparations. They began to build a stock of atomic bombs, to develop the far more destructive hydrogen bomb, and a system of delivering such bombs. Quantities of armaments were also sent to countries such as Greece and Turkey, where communism was thought to be a threat, or which could form a bulwark (defence) against the spread of Russian communism. Aid was given to these countries only on condition that they reduced tariffs, controlled prices and agreed to send strategic materials to the USA, while denying them to communist countries. A hysterical fear of communism which was stirred up by Senator McCarthy, swept over America. Thousands of people, many of them in important positions, came under suspicion, and many were disgraced or dismissed.

NATO, SEATO and the Warsaw Pact

Meanwhile at the United Nations the USA was frustrated by opposition by Russia, which vetoed many United Nations suggestions. In 1949 therefore the USA formed the North Atlantic Treaty Organization (NATO) with Canada, Britain, France, Italy, Norway, Denmark, Holland and Belgium, and later, West Germany, Greece and Turkey, as a defensive alliance against possible communist aggression. A few years later Russia replied with the Warsaw Pact, an alliance of all the eastern European communist countries. The USA had already signed a treaty of mutual assistance with all the Latin American countries in 1947, with Indo-China in 1950, and with New Zealand and Australia in 1951. In 1954 the South East Asia Treaty Organization was formed by the USA with Britain, France, Australia, New Zealand, Pakistan, Thailand and the Philippines. This was known as SEATO.

Peaceful co-existence?

In 1953 Stalin, the Russian dictator died. Khrushchev, who became premier in his place in 1955 realized that a nuclear war between Russia and America would be so destructive that human civilization, and possibly all human life on the earth might be destroyed. Instead of maintaining that there must be unending enmity between communism and capitalism, until one was destroyed, he suggested that both could live side by side in 'peaceful co-existence'. There would still be rivalry, said Khrushchev, and capitalism would still come to an end, but through the realization by people everywhere that communism was the best way of life and government.

Suspense continued, however, and in 1960, just when a conference had been arranged between Khrushchev and President Eisenhower of the USA, an American 'spy plane' was shot down over central Russia. The conference was called off. Rivalry was intensified, and largely took the form of the 'space race'. In 1957 Russia launched the first earth satellite or sputnik. America was shocked to find that Russia was ahead of her in space research. Each country devoted vast resources to the construction of satellites and launching devices. In 1961 Yuri Gagarin, a Russian, was the first man to circle the earth in space in a satellite.

In 1962 Russia attempted to install a missile base in communist Cuba. The Americans demanded their withdrawal. The world seemed on the brink of a nuclear war. President Kennedy of America took a firm line, and Khrushchev agreed to remove the missiles. The following year a direct telephone communication (a 'hot line') was established between the heads of the Russian and American governments, in case of emergency, so that the two most powerful people in the world could discuss any crisis that might arise in world affairs. Perhaps the fear of the terrible effects of a nuclear war will prevent such a war breaking out.

Exercises and things to do

Cuban stamp to commemorate the Russians landing on the moon in 1978.

1 Write out, filling in the blanks. One – stands for each missing letter.

After the Second World War most of – – – – – was exhausted. In – – – – – many millions of lives had been lost and homes, railways and – – – – – – – – had been badly damaged; but in the USA there had been no – – – – – – and the country could produce – – – – quantities of – – – – –. Through the – – – – – – – – Plan, America agreed to provide the – – – – – – – – countries with – – – – – so that they could – – – the things they needed, and so keep the – – – – – – – – people and their – – – – – – – – with plenty of – – – –. America was thus the leader of the – – – – – – – – – or – – – – World as they called it.

The Russians built up their strength as – – – – – – – as possible and united the – – – – – – – European – – – – – – – – countries which she had helped to come to power, in the – – – – – – – –. Russia feared the – – – – – – – – – world, and the USA feared the – – – – – – – – – world, and between the two there was an – – – – – – – – – – – and what came to be called the – – – – – – –. Both sides built up huge – – – – – – – – –.

2 The heads and tails of these statements have been mixed. Write them out correctly.

(a) The Marshall Plan
(b) The iron curtain
(c) NATO
(d) The Cominform
(e) Kennedy
(f) The cold war
(g) Khrushchev
(h) The Warsaw Pact

(1) was a Russian arrangement to help the communist countries to work together.
(2) was rivalry between capitalist countries and communist countries.
(3) was a communist alliance.
(4) was an American offer of money to help the countries of Europe.
(5) was a Russian leader.
(6) was the obstacle to friendly contact between communist and capitalist countries.
(7) was president of the USA.
(8) was an alliance of America and western Europeans.

The division of Europe into armed blocks. The Warsaw Pact nations are controlled by Russia.

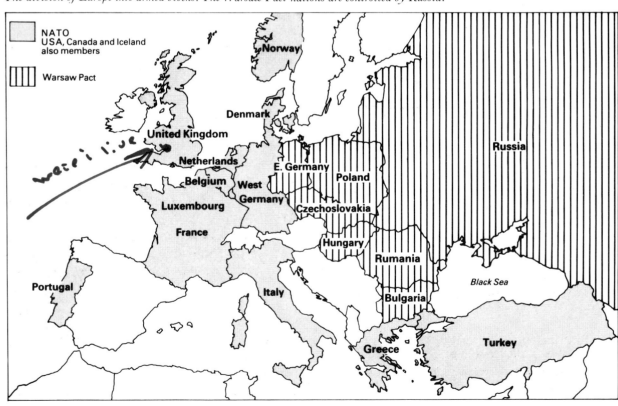

The 1960s were a decade of rivalry in space between the USA and USSR. Russian airman, Yuri Gagarin, was the first man in space but the Americans succeeded in putting the first man on the moon.

In 1975 there was a joint Russian American project where they co-operated to test docking systems in space.

3 *Statements of fact* Write out the four statements in each group in what you think is their order of importance or interest. Say in each group why you decided to put one particular statement first.

(a) After the Second World War
   (1) Germany was divided into occupied zones.
   (2) Britain and her west European allies were exhausted.
   (3) the USA was stronger whilst almost all the rest of the world was weaker.
   (4) the USA wanted to prevent depression so that she could counter the spread of communism.

(b) The USA
   (1) agreed to supply western Europe with Marshall Aid.
   (2) made treaties with all the Latin American countries.
   (3) made the NATO alliance with the countries on both sides of the North Atlantic.
   (4) formed SEATO, an alliance of countries interested in south-east Asia.

(c) Russian suspicion of the West
   (1) led to the cold war.
   (2) made her bring down the iron curtain.
   (3) led her to refuse to share in the Marshall Plan.
   (4) was relaxed when Khrushchev suggested the idea of peaceful co-existence.

4 *The right order* Write these out in the order in which they happened.

(a) The Warsaw Pact was formed.
(b) The Marshall Plan was agreed.
(c) Russia launched the first satellite.
(d) NATO was formed.

5 *The main idea* Write out the one sentence which tells what you think is the main idea of this topic.

(a) The USA maintained her prosperity and her leadership of the non-communist world.
(b) Russia became the communist leading power, opposed to the capitalist world.
(c) Russia and the USA were rivals.
(d) The cold war affected much of the world.

6 Look at the map and complete this chart.

Divided Europe	
NATO countries	Warsaw Pact countries
Italy	*Hungary*

7 Explain the meaning of the following:

(a) the Marshall Plan
(b) the Iron Curtain
(c) peaceful co-existence

8 Copy this map of the world and label the countries. Then try to explain why the USA demanded that Russia remove missiles from Cuba.

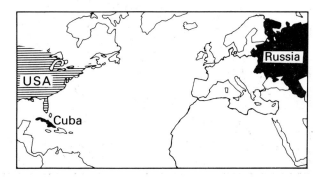

20 Empire into commonwealth

When the League of Nations was formed in 1919, the British dominions, Canada, South Africa, Australia and New Zealand were admitted to membership of the League in their own right. It was clear that they were no longer colonies. In 1931 the Statute of Westminster, passed by the British government, recognized that these countries were now sovereign states, with complete control of their relations with other countries, as well as self-government at home. They still continued to be members of the British commonwealth, and recognized the monarch as its head.

During the Second World War, all these dominions decided to support Britain, and declared war on Germany within a few days of the beginning of the war. Only Ireland, which had gained its freedom only after rebellion and civil war, decided to remain neutral. Canada produced great quantities of war materials, and made a big loan to Britain to help her after the war. The Canadians took a prominent part in forming the North Atlantic Treaty Organization. Australia and New Zealand contributed many troops to the fighting in many parts of the world. Only in South Africa was there much opposition to entry into the war.

Australia and New Zealand had been nervous of possible Japanese aggression during much of the twentieth century. In the Second World War they realized that Britain could no longer be relied upon to protect them. It was the American fleets and air forces which defeated the Japanese, and Australia and New Zealand turned increasingly to the USA for leadership. They joined the South East Asia Treaty Organization, and sent troops to assist the USA in the war in Vietnam.

India

In 1939 when the Second World War broke out, the Viceroy of India declared that India was at war with Germany. He had not consulted the Indian people, who resented the fact that Britain, who claimed to be fighting the war to defend freedom and democracy, did not give freedom and democracy to India. There were strikes against the war. Leaders of this opposition who were opposed to the use of violence were imprisoned. Mahatma Gandhi led the Indians in the demand that the British should quit India completely. Although some Indians volunteered to serve in the army against Japan, discontent continued.

In 1945 the new British Labour government promised to give India complete independence. There were 350 million Hindus and 100 million Muslims, and their leaders could not agree on the form that independent India should take. There were widespread riots, but in 1947 Gandhi, the Hindu leader, and Jinnah, leader of the Muslims, met and agreed to the creation of two separate independent states: Hindu India and Muslim Pakistan. They continued to be members of the commonwealth.

For centuries India had been a land of poor peasants. The war made the position worse. In

Mahatma Gandhi led the Indians towards independence but Nehru became India's first Prime Minister in 1947 when British rule ended. This picture shows Gandhi with his grand-daughters on his way to prayer shortly before his assassination in 1948.

1947 the average income of the Indians was only one sixteenth of that of the average Briton. The average expectation of life of a newly born Indian was thirty-two years, less than half that of a Briton. Over 250 million Indians depended upon agriculture to live. Less than one third of the children of primary school age were able to go to school, and only one seventh of the adults could read or write. In most parts of India there was only one doctor for every 25,000 people. Only a quarter of the cities had a safe water supply, and less than half had any electricity.

Having gained independence, the Indian people expected that their living conditions would be improved, but it was an overwhelming task. The government under Nehru was anxious to copy what they thought was good in the western system, and also gain what help they could from the communist world. So India was to be neither all capitalist nor all socialist. There were votes for all, and freedom for all political parties. There were plans to encourage industry, so that a smaller proportion of the population depended upon agriculture, to raise the national income, and to introduce free education for all boys and girls between the ages of six and eleven. Bad harvests, famines, disputes with Pakistan and China, and a rapidly increasing population made it difficult to raise the standard of living as quickly as was hoped.

In foreign affairs India had been one of the leading neutral powers, doing her best to prevent the whole world from dividing into two opposing camps. The Indians have tried to adopt a friendly attitude towards communist Russia and communist China, in spite of trouble on the frontier, and on the whole have been able to maintain some influence for peaceful progress.

Independence spreads

The colonies of Ceylon and Burma became independent of Britain in 1948 and Burma decided to leave the commonwealth. Meanwhile the demand for independence was moving to Africa, and one after another Britain's African

colonies became sovereign states, some peacefully, others only after terrorism and war. Ghana, which had been the Gold Coast was freed in 1957, Nigeria in 1960, Sierra Leone in 1961, Uganda in 1962, Kenya and Malawi in 1963, Tanganyika and Zambia (the old Northern Rhodesia) in 1964 and Gambia in 1965. Elsewhere, Cyprus was freed in 1961, Jamaica and Trinidad in 1962, Malta in 1964. Malaya joined with other south-east Asian colonies to form Malaysia in 1963. All these became members of the United Nations, and took an important part in expressing the 'Afro-Asian' point of view. This was utterly opposed to the South African policy of apartheid (keeping black and white people apart). At a conference of commonwealth prime ministers in 1961, there was such criticism of South Africa, particularly from the representatives of Ghana and India, that South Africa withdrew from the commonwealth and became a republic.

The 300,000 white settlers of Southern Rhodesia, who alone formed the government of the colony demanded independence, but the British government refused to grant this until the 4,000,000 Africans were given a full share in the government. This the existing white government refused, and in 1965, under Ian Smith, illegally declared their independence. They had no intention of moving towards the possibility of an African government. 'Not in a thousand years,' said Mr Smith.

Britain, supported by the United Nations, imposed sanctions upon Rhodesia, cutting her off from international trade, in an attempt to force her to give the African majority the right to choose the government. Many of the Africans took to arms, but it was not until 1981, after years of 'freedom fighter' attacks that freedom did come to Rhodesia, under the new name of Zimbabwe, with a government composed mainly of Africans, but with a certain number of whites guaranteed for a few years. Mr Ian Smith led the small white group in the Zimbabwe parliament.

83

Exercises and things to do

1 Write out, filling in the blanks. One – stands for each missing letter.

After the First World War, four British –––––––, South Africa, –––––, –––––––– and New ––––––– were treated like independent states and given membership of the League of–––––––. This was recognized by the ––––––– government in 1931 in the –––––––of–––––––––.

During the Second World War the people of –––––, led by ––––––– –––––––, demanded their –––––––, and in 1947 the country became ––––––––––, and divided into two states, ––––– and –––––––. Other colonies in Asia, ––––––– and ––––– became independent in –––––.

After 1957 most of the colonies in Africa, including –––––––, –––––, ––––––––––, the –––– –––––, and Northern ––––––––– (now Zambia) gained their independence. Nearly all of them continued to be members of the –––––––––––.

Belgian Congonese workmen celebrate independence by toppling the statue of the late King Albert of the Belgians – Stanleyville, April 1960.

2 The heads and tails of these statements have been mixed. Write them out correctly.

(a) Mahatma Gandhi	(1) became head of the Indian government.
(b) Ghana	(2) is the new name for Northern Rhodesia.
(c) Nehru	(3) led the Muslims in India.
(d) Burma	(4) is the name for the Gold Coast.
(e) Zambia	(5) decided not to be a member of the commonwealth.
(f) South Africa	(6) declared its independence illegally.
(g) Jinnah	(7) led the Indians in their demand for freedom.
(h) Rhodesia	(8) withdrew from the commonwealth because of criticism of apartheid.

3 *Statements of fact* Write out the four statements in each group in what you think is their order of importance or interest. Say in each group why you decided to put one particular statement first.

(a) The Statute of Westminster
   (1) was passed in 1931.
   (2) recognized that the dominions were independent states.
   (3) placed Canada, South Africa, Australia and New Zealand on an equal footing with Britain.
   (4) gave the dominions the right to control relations with other countries.

(b) During the Second World War
   (1) the Indian people were dissatisfied because they had not been free to decide whether they wished to enter the war.
   (2) Canada took an important part in war strategy.
   (3) the dominions fought alongside Britain against Germany and Japan.
   (4) some of the dominions realized that Britain could not protect them adequately.

(c) After 1945
   (1) Britain began to prepare the other colonies for independence.
   (2) first the Asian and then the African colonies gained independence.
   (3) most British colonies continued to be members of the commonwealth.
   (4) criticism of its apartheid policy forced South Africa to leave the commonwealth.

4 *The right order* Write these out in the order in which they happened.

(a) Ghana became independent.
(b) The Statute of Westminster.
(c) India became independent.
(d) The dominions declared war on Germany.

5 *The main idea* Write out the one sentence which tells what you think is the main idea of this topic.

(a) The demand for independence became more insistent after 1945.
(b) The British colonies have been transformed into independent states.
(c) The British empire has become a common-wealth of free nations.
(d) Most of the British dominions played an important part in the Second World War.

6 Why do you think the colonies wished to be free from British rule?

7 Using other books (such as an atlas) make a list of those countries in the commonwealth. Which countries have left the commonwealth?

8 Do you think that the commonwealth serves a purpose?

9 Choose one of the following countries – India, New Zealand, Jamaica, Kenya, Pakistan, Australia and South Africa. Collect pictures and information about its people.

Front page of 'Evening Standard' on the day when Ian Smith declared UDI – Unilateral Declaration of Independence.

Evening Standard

WEST END FINAL
CLOSING PRICES

Mekay QUALITY SHIRTS

43,979   1, 196   55

Sumrie 210 PICCADILLY near the CIRCUS
Sumrie clothes are good—really good

UDI—Smith goes it alone

BRITAIN SLAMS TOUGH SANCTIONS ON THE 'REBELS'

No more tobacco buying

'REASON HAD FLED THE SCENE . . .'

Evening Standard Parliamentary Reporter

The British Government is embarking immediately on drastic and comprehensive sanctions — almost everything short of military force — to bring the now rebellious, illegal and outlawed regime of Mr. Ian Smith in Rhodesia to its knees.

In a grim and determined statement to a packed and tense House of Commons this afternoon Mr. Wilson announced emergency action aimed at restoring the rule of law, legal Government, and, as he put it, freedom in Rhodesia.

Mr. Wilson then announced: "All British aid will cease."

ARMS exports will be banned.

Rhodesia has been removed from the STERLING area and special exchange control restrictions will be applied. Exports of U.K. capital to Rhodesia will not be allowed.

Rhodesia will no longer have access to the London CAPITAL MARKET and the Export Credits guarantee department will give no further cover for EXPORTS to Rhodesia.

The Ottawa agreement, governing trading agreements is suspended.

Labour cheers

Rhodesia is suspended forthwith from the Commonwealth PREFERENCE area and goods from Rhodesia will no longer receive preferential treatment on entering the UK

CENSORSHIP FOLLOWS THE BREAKAWAY

SALISBURY, Thursday. — Mr. Ian Smith, in a voice trembling at times with emotion, today defied Britain and seized independence for Rhodesia in the first rebellion of its kind since America broke away as a colony in 1776.

His unilateral declaration of independence came in a drama-charged broadcast to the nation of 217,000 Whites and 4,000,000 Africans.

Mr. Smith said the "end of the road had been reached" in negotiations. But his action did not mean that the principles enshrined in the present constitution would be torn up. The Union Jack would continue to fly in Rhodesia and the National Anthem would continue to be played, he said.

He proclaimed unswerving loyalty to the Crown. "God save the Queen," he said.

Then shortly after the broadcast the Government announced the imposition of censorship. The announcement said no one shall print or publish any publication without prior authority of the Director of Information.

A fuller report—PAGE SIXTEEN.

CENSORSHIP DETAILS
PAGE SEVENTEEN

Smith's proclamation
PAGE EIGHTEEN

THE CITY TAKES IT CALMLY

The news from Rhodesia was taken calmly in the City today. On the Stock Exchange the immediate reaction was to mark all shares down. But the falls in most cases only amounted to a few pence.

Whitehall flashed good news

The news from Rhodesia was to the City. Against most expectations our trade gap—was and sell overseas—narrowed very slightly in October.

Most encouragingly, exports showed a further small increase.
—See Page THREE.

QUEEN SUSPENDS SMITH

—and his Ministers

SALISBURY, Thursday.—Mr. Smith and all his ministers are now suspended from office —on the Queen's instructions.

The Rhodesian Governor, Sir Humphrey Gibbs, announced this immediately after Mr. Smith declared independence.

But what was not immediately clear was how the Governor could implement the Royal Instructions; and how the country's government is to be carried on in the critical interim period.

Sir Humphrey, in his prepared statement, said:

" The government have made an unconstitutional declaration of independence.

" I have received the following message from Her Majesty's Secretary of State for Commonwealth Relations.

" I have it in command from Her Majesty to inform you that it is Her Majesty's pleasure that in the event of an unconstitutional declaration of independence. Mr. Ian Smith and other persons holding office as Ministers of the Government of Southern Rhodesia or as Deputy Ministers cease to hold office.

" I am commanded by Her Majesty to instruct you in that event to convey Her Majesty's pleasure in this matter to Mr. Smith and otherwise to publish it in such a manner as you may deem fit."

The Governor then called on all citizens of Rhodesia "to refrain from all acts which would further the objectives of the illegal authorities."

He added: "Subject to that is the duty of all citizens to maintain law and order in the country and carry on with their normal tasks."

Sir Humphrey said his instructions applied "equally to the judiciary, the armed forces, the police and the public services."

It's here now, the new WOLSELEY 1100

test-drive it today–ring Eustace Watkins

There's no mistaking the Wolseley touch—it's obvious in every stylish inch of this superb new car. But you can see for yourself—the real test comes when you drive it. To do just that—ring Eustace Watkins. Twin carburetters; front disc brakes. Hydrolastic suspension and Wolseley luxury combine to make this one of the outstanding cars of the year. Price: £794. 7. 1. (inc. Purchase Tax).

EUSTACE WATKINS

What do you know?

All the answers to these questions are somewhere in this book. Page numbers are given to help you.

1 The first man in space was

(a) Yuri Gagarin
(b) John Glenn
(c) Neil Armstrong.
(Clue: see page 79)

2 A turnpike was

(a) an entry to a sports ground
(b) a road
(c) a means of cooking meat.
(Clue: see page 13)

3 The leader of the German Nazi Party was

(a) the Kaiser
(b) Adolf Hitler
(c) Rudolf Hess.
(Clue: see page 70)

4 1926 was the year of

(a) the Great Exhibition
(b) the Great Depression
(c) the General Strike.
(Clue: see page 63)

5 The following person was assassinated at Sarajevo:

(a) Abraham Lincoln
(b) Mahatma Gandhi
(c) Archduke Franz Ferdinand of Austria.
(Clue: see page 54)

6 The Yorkshireman who fought against slavery was

(a) John Metcalfe
(b) James Cook
(c) William Wilberforce.
(Clue: see page 24)

7 The international organization set up after the First World War was

(a) NATO
(b) the League of Nations
(c) the United Nations.
(Clue: see page 5)

8 The leader of Italy in the Second World War was

(a) Garibaldi
(b) Mussolini
(c) Mazzini.
(Clue: see page 70)

9 The nation defeated by Prussia in 1871 was

(a) Austria
(b) Russia
(c) France.
(Clue: see page 37)

10 The American president who introduced the New Deal was

(a) Franklin D. Roosevelt
(b) Woodrow Wilson
(c) Harry Truman.
(Clue: see page 67)

11 The leader of the Chinese Communist revolution was

(a) Ho Chi Minh
(b) Mao Tse-Tung
(c) U Thant.
(Clue: see page 78)

12 Which of the following fought the British in South Africa?

(a) The Boxers
(b) The Boers
(c) The Fenians.
(Clue: see page 46)

13 A Viceroy ruled

(a) Canada
(b) Burma
(c) India.
(*Clue: see page 82*)

14 The atomic bomb was dropped on

(a) Tokyo
(b) Berlin
(c) Hiroshima.
(*Clue: see page 73*)

Answers on page 96.

15 Look at the two pictures of a railway station in Victorian times and a twentieth century airport lounge. What are the similarities and differences in

(a) clothing
(b) types of people
(c) hairstyles
(d) the surroundings
(e) methods of transport
(f) where people are likely to be going?

16 Choose one person or group of people from the picture of the railway station and describe what they look like, what they are doing, where you think they might be going, and why.

21 Conflicts around the world

*The UNO
symbol*

Israel and the near east

There are several regions in the world where great changes have taken place, or where there are difficult problems or dangerous situations. For a long time the Arabs of the Middle East had been under foreign rule, and when, after two world wars which were supposed to be fought in the cause of freedom, some of them were still under foreign control, there was great resentment. This increased when in 1948 the United Nations decided to give the Jews a national home in Palestine, which had long been regarded as an Arab land.

In the distant past, for a thousand years, Palestine had been the land of the Jews, or Israelites. They were driven out by the Romans nearly two thousand years ago, and were scattered about the world, without any country of their own, and they still looked back to Palestine as their homeland, although the Arabs had lived there for many centuries.

Egypt and the Suez Canal

As one of the Arab states, Egypt had objected to the setting up of the Jewish state of Israel, and would not allow Israeli ships to use the Suez Canal. With American help, Egypt was planning a large new dam on the Nile at Assuan, but in 1956 the Americans withdrew their offer of a big loan. President Nasser of Egypt therefore decided to nationalize the Suez Canal, and use the profits to finance the dam. Britain and France were very annoyed with Nasser as they both had shares in it, and they decided to take over the canal, and get rid of Nasser at the same time. The enmity between Israel and Egypt came in very useful: Israel was encouraged to attack Egypt, and the British and French then sent an ultimatum to both sides, calling for a cease fire, and ordering both armies to retire to a line sixteen kilometres from the canal, so that it could be occupied by British and French forces. Israel accepted the ultimatum, and pushed on rapidly, as her troops had not yet reached the line sixteen kilometres from the canal. Egypt, who had been attacked, and in whose territory the canal was situated, naturally refused to comply, whereupon the British and French began bombing Egypt, and troops were landed.

At the United Nations, Britain and France were condemned by almost everybody, and called upon to stop the attack. They did so, and the Egyptians were left in control of the canal. The state of war between Israel and the Arab states did not end, and this dangerous situation has continued to threaten to lead to a more general war. The Arab countries of the Middle East have the largest oil-fields in the world, and some people in America fear that Russia might try to gain control of them, since supplies in the whole world will soon be running out. America is tempted to build up military forces in the region, and this might lead to a clash between these two super powers.

South Africa and apartheid

The biggest problem in Africa is in South Africa where the white government operates the policy of apartheid. This means keeping the races separate. Thus there is a white South Africa, and a number of areas which are set aside for the Africans and the 'coloureds', people of mixed race. These are called 'Bantustans'. In these 'Bantustans' the South African government says the native peoples can live their own life under their own laws, and become self-governing states in a South African commonwealth. But in white South Africa the four million whites have twelve million African and coloured people working for them, but these workers do not have the right to vote or take part in the government. The white territory contains seven eighths of the whole country. The remaining one eighth is for eight million Africans.

The division is even more unequal. The white state includes all the large cities, the seaports, the harbours, power lines and major irrigation schemes. It contains the enormously rich gold mines, the diamond mines, the coal mines and the best and most fertile farmlands. The Bantu 'homelands' consist of over two hundred small separate areas. They are in primitive rural land, soil eroded and under-developed.

Most of the men whose families are in the Bantu lands, work in the white man's factories, mines and farms, which are usually hundreds of kilometres away from their so-called 'homelands', while the women and children scrape what little living they can from the poor and overcrowded 'native reserves'.

The United Nations has called upon South

Africa to give up their policy of apartheid. Most of the African independent states have formed the Organization of African Unity, to enable them to work together, and to help those Africans who are still struggling for their freedom, and are becoming less and less willing to put up with the injustice of apartheid.

One of the ugliest sides of apartheid was shown at Sharpeville in 1963 when white South African police took action against a black crowd.

China

In 1949 the Chinese Communist Party gained control of all China. At first they obtained help from communist Russia, while America would have nothing to do with the new Chinese government. Then there were quarrels between the two great communist countries, and in the 1970s America began to hope that China might be an ally against Russia, and opened up friendly relations. The Chinese have made their own atomic and hydrogen bombs, and there is much doubt over what this vast country with a quarter of the world's population will do in the future.

Latin America

The twentieth century has brought great changes in Latin America. Population is growing rapidly, and huge cities have been built, with large modern buildings where many wealthy people live in the grand manner, but where hundreds of thousands live in poverty, in miserable slums and shanty towns. In most Latin American countries there have been frequent revolutions, and most of them are ruled by dictators who often maintain their rule with the help of the army.

The USA has taken an increasingly important part in Latin American affairs. United States banks and business houses opened branches in most Latin American cities, and gained a great deal of control over trade and industry. The USA is very nervous about the spread of communism, particularly in America, and encourages any rulers who are likely to be anti-communist.

Unity in Europe

After the Second World War most of eastern Europe, including eastern Germany, came under the control of Russia. Many western Europeans feared that Russia had designs upon the rest of Europe, so some looked to America for help, but other westerners resented the growing influence of the USA upon the western world. All were agreed, however, that the countries of western Europe must work together, and must never again go to war with one another.

Several European countries wanted to work more closely together in other political and economic matters. In 1956 the Treaty of Rome was drawn up, creating the Common Market, or European Economic Community (EEC), composed of Belgium, France, Holland, Italy, Luxemburg and Western Germany. The aim was to get rid of customs duties between members, and to agree on common duties on goods from outside the Market. All six agreed to work towards similar farming and transport systems, and to the free movement of people between member countries.

In the early 1970s Britain, Denmark and Ireland joined the Common Market, and later it was agreed that Greece, Spain and Portugal should join. The various members do not always find it easy to come to agreements, but at least they can discuss them, and do not go to war to settle their differences.

Exercises and things to do

1 Write out, filling in the blanks. One – stands for each missing letter.

There was trouble and sometimes ––– in Palestine between the –––– who have set up the state of ––––––, and the ––––– who claim that it is their land.

In South Africa there is trouble between the ––––– government and the –––––––– workers who, because of the policy of –––––––––, cannot ––– with white people, and are often separated from their ––––– and ––––––––.

In Latin America there are great differences between –––– and ––––. Most of the countries are ruled by –––––––– and there are often revolutions.

2 The heads and tails of these statements have been mixed. Write them out correctly.

(a) Apartheid	(1) is an agreement between European countries.
(b) Bantustans	(2) are slum areas in big cities.
(c) The Common Market	(3) is the system of keeping white and coloured people apart.
(d) Shanty towns	(4) are areas in South Africa where many of the black people have to live.

3 *Statements of fact* Write out the four statements in each group in their order of importance or interest. Say in each group why you decided to put one particular statement first.

(a) After the Second World War peace was threatened by
  (1) the making of the state of Israel in Palestine.
  (2) Egypt's nationalization of the Suez Canal.
  (3) South Africa's treatment of coloured people through apartheid.
  (4) China's making of atomic bombs.

(b) Actions which it was hoped would help to avoid war were the
  (1) formation of the United Nations.
  (2) setting up of the Organization of African Unity.
  (3) formation of the European Common Market.
  (4) interest of the USA in Latin American affairs.

4 *The right order* Write these out in the order in which they happened.

(a) The formation of the state of Israel.
(b) the drawing up of the Treaty of Rome.
(c) The communist control of all China.
(d) Britain joined the EEC.

This cartoon was drawn at the time United Nations was formed in 1945. The cartoonist is obviously doubtful about the effectiveness of the organization.

Presidents Nixon (USA) and Brezhnev (USSR) supplied 'transfusions' of arms and supplies to Arabs and Israelis during the 1970s.

5 *The main idea* Write out the one sentence which tells what you think is the main idea of this topic.

(a) Countries in many parts of the world were interested in making arrangements to work together.

(b) People in various parts of the world were trying to gain freedom.

(c) The United Nations has tried to solve some of the world's problems.

(d) The world's main problems arise from a struggle for national independence, and for the fair treatment of coloured people.

6 Copy this outline map of Europe. Label the countries. Shade in all the countries which already belong to the European Economic Community or will be joining it.

1 Portugal, 2 Spain, 3 France, 4 Luxembourg,
5 Belgium, 6 Britain, 7 Ireland, 8 Holland,
9 West Germany, 10 East Germany, 11 Denmark,
12 Norway, 13 Sweden, 14 Poland,
15 Czechoslovakia, 16 Austria, 17 Switzerland,
18 Hungary, 19 Yugoslavia, 20 Rumania,
21 Bulgaria, 22 Greece, 23 Italy, 24 Russia.

The British and French invaded Egypt in 1956 in response to Nasser's seizure of the Suez Canal. They were supported by Israel but their action angered the USA.

The Evening News

NO. 23,282   LONDON, MONDAY, NOVEMBER 5, 1956   TWOPENCE

AT A GLANCE —

● ROYAL variety show to-night cancelled, after the Queen's decision not to attend, in view of international situation.

● GENERAL ASSEMBLY adopted plan for U.N. police force in Middle E--t by 57 votes to none, with 19 abstentions (P8)

● AIR MINISTRY denied Egyptian charge of terror bombing and said Allied air forces had taken "scrupulous care." (P3)

Part of the crowd that waited in Downing-street to-day, before being moved by the police.

The Crisis News

○ BRITISH invasion forces met some very tough fighting, said General Sir Charles Keightley, C-in-C Middle East (P1)

○ PARATROOPS flew in off diet of orangeade hard-boiled eggs and barley sugar, said Kent squadron leader (P3)

○ THIRTY-TWO people were accused at Bowstreet after "no war" uproar in Trafalgar-square and Whitehall (P2)

SKYMEN LAND—SOME VERY TOUGH FIGHTING

But Red Devils Firmly Established: Port Said Airport is Captured and French Troops Seize Bridges

THE QUEEN CANCELS PALLADIUM VISIT

Royal Variety Show is Off

THE Royal Variety Show at the London Palladium to-night has been cancelled because of the international situation.

Earlier this afternoon, it was stated that the Queen had decided she would be unable to attend, because of the international situation.

Neither Queen Elizabeth, the Queen Mother, nor Princess Margaret would be present.

The performance was to be in aid of the Variety Artistes' Benevolent Fund.

MESSAGE
From the Palace

Later Mr. Harry Marlow, secretary of the Variety Artistes' Benevolent Fund, said: "Buckingham Palace informed me that

SECOND WAVE DROPS TO SOUTH: CASUALTIES LOW

A SECOND WAVE OF PARATROOPS DROPPED ON THE SUEZ CANAL ZONE THIS AFTERNOON. BRITISH SKYMEN IN THE FIRST ASSAULT HAD ALREADY CAPTURED PORT SAID AIRPORT. FRENCH PARATROOPS SEIZED TWO BRIDGES SPANNING THE CANAL BACKWATERS SOUTH OF PORT SAID.

The second drop was announced by General Sir Charles Keightley, commanding the Anglo-French forces. He said French skymen were involved.

"It is a big drop, landing close to the other one. If all goes well it will link up and form a combined front south of Port Said," he reported at the Allied H.Q. in Cyprus eight hours after the original landings.

The French were due to land at 3 p.m. local time. The general said the British and French "have had some very tough fighting."

General Sir Charles Keightley.

Skymen Knock Out Tanks

SUEZ: 'THE THIRD WAVE GOES IN'

Beirut.—Damascus Radio said third wave of parachutists landed near Port Said one evening.

Of Cyprus Gen. Keightley said Brigadier Butler had reported "Gamil airfield now serviceable for helicopters. Resistance slackened.

French relief in possession of bridge"—A.P. and B.U.P.

LLOYD ON U.N. CALL TO BRITAIN

Mr. Selwyn Lloyd in Commons statement on Middle East made U.N. Secretary-General's message to him a Government disclosing effort to reestablish peace in the Middle East. American and calling for an early cessation of action in area by S.Y.M. C.I.F.T. accepted

Chargeness had replied that if the Allies achieved their purpose the two Governments had stated carefully and welcomed an international police force, pending enforcement

The thumbs-up sign and smiles of confidence as paratroops set off from Cyprus for Suez.

Seaborne Army is Awaiting the 'Off'

U.S. FLEET NEARS TROUBLE ZONE

22 Modern world problems

There are some problems which concern almost the whole world.

A new industrial revolution

The modern world is seeing a new industrial revolution, which is changing conditions of life almost everywhere. In many cases the first use to be made of new forces is for warfare and destruction: the immediate result of the harnessing of nuclear energy was the dropping of two atomic bombs on Japanese cities, killing 200,000 men, women and children. At first the USA alone had the secret of making such bombs, but within a few years Russia, Britain and France were also making them, and in the 1960s China exploded her first nuclear bombs. Today we cannot be sure what other countries possess these bombs. Vast sums are spent on developing more destructive types of weapons, and on building up huge stocks. If these deadly weapons are used, they could lead to the end of civilization, if not of mankind itself.

Meanwhile technologists have been producing electronic computers which make calculations a thousand times faster than any human brain. This gives a promise that in the future not only will much of the boring and unpleasant work be performed by machines, but much of the control of the machines too, and a great deal of clerical work will not need human labour. Will this mean that there will be unemployment and poverty for some, and almost unlimited leisure and luxury for others? Or will it be possible to share out the leisure time and the increased production fairly among all the people?

The population explosion

By improving health, and so reducing the death rate, science has led to a population explosion. There are more than four thousand million people in the world today, and the population is increasing ever more rapidly. (See diagram on pages 6–7.) In thirty years there will be twice as many people as there are now. How will they be fed? Already half the world's people do not have enough to eat.

What is the remedy? One way is the limiting of families. Parents can be encouraged not to have large families, and this is happening in some countries. A second is to introduce better methods of producing food.

Biologists have produced new types of food plants which make it possible to reap harvests in areas so dry or so cold that it would have been out of the question a few years ago. New types and larger quantities of fertilizers can greatly increase the amount of food produced in a given area. Deep under the Sahara Desert are vast supplies of water, and this is now being brought to the surface. Unfortunately, no sooner had the water begun to create fertile fields than the French tested their nuclear bombs there, and poisonous fall-out began to contaminate everything.

Unfortunately, in many of the most overpopulated parts of the world, where the need is greatest, the people are too poor to buy the fertilizers and machinery needed for these improvements. Many cannot even afford to buy fuel for cooking, and they dry animal dung and burn that. There is then no manure for the crops. It is a vicious circle: poor crops mean poor people; poor people cannot buy fertilizers; lack of fertilizers means poor crops.

It therefore appears that the only remedy is for the richer countries to supply the poor ones with the fertilizers and machinery they need. But the people in the wealthy countries who have money to lend want interest on their money, and the poor countries cannot afford to pay it. The USA and many other countries have sent food at various times to help countries in need, but no real worldwide solution to the problem has been attempted. Governments of richer countries say their taxes are already too high, and so they can spare only very small sums for 'foreign aid'. And so the poor countries go on getting poorer, and the rich countries richer; and all are becoming overcrowded.

Race and colour

Another world-wide problem is that of finding some way in which people of different race and colour can live peacefully and happily together. In the USA there are about thirty million Negroes living among 190 million whites. In Britain some two million blacks and Asians live among fifty million whites, and in many other lands there are laws limiting the number of coloured immigrants. There is often much 'racial feeling': the coloured people feel that they are not treated fairly; the white people say they do not like the coloured people's ways.

There is a tendency among some whites to feel superior to coloured people, but coloured people are less impressed by the whites with their depressions, world wars, atom bombs and frantic scramble for profits.

A few white citizens are determined to prevent coloured people from exercising their right to vote at elections; but others are doing all they can to secure for them all the equal rights to which they are entitled. With modern methods of travel and communication, there is far more mixing of races than in the past, and the problem of getting all races to live peacefully together is becoming more urgent.

East v West or North v South?

The modern world is still a divided world, but its divisions are world-wide. There is co-operation between some states and rivalry between others, but there is a rivalry of ideas, or what are called ideologies. The two main ones are capitalism and communism.

Both capitalists and communists claim that their system gives people freedom, and capitalists refer to their part of the world as the 'free world' while the communists call theirs the 'people's democracies'. The state of tension between these two groups is known as the Cold War, between East and West. There is by no means unity between all capitalists or all communists. The Second World War began between rival capitalist countries; in the 1960s there was violent disagreement between the Russian and the Chinese communists.

The USA is the leader of the capitalist world and Russia leads the communists. A third group, the neutral world is composed mainly of countries which have recently become independent. They do not wish to become involved in the Cold War, but may take help from either quarter. Some people think that the greatest division of the world

Although many people in the world do not have enough to eat, the richer countries waste large amounts of food every year. This picture shows a mountain of tomatoes in Florida, which have been thrown away because they are not attractive enough to be displayed in shops.

today is not that between east and west, but between north and south, that is, between the rich and developed capitalists and communists of Europe, Russia, Japan and North America, and the poor undeveloped world of the south.

So it becomes clear that we live in a world which is constantly changing, and with each new change, comes a new set of problems.

Exercises and things to do

1 Write out, filling in the blanks. One – stands for each missing letter.

The modern world is one of rapid – – – – –, and new – – – – – – – and dangers. – – – – – – – weapons could lead to the end of – – – – – – – – – – –. Electronic – – – – – – – – will greatly – – – – – – the amount of – – – – that will have to be done by human beings. This could lead to – – – – – – – – – – and – – – – – – for many people.

The population of the world is – – – – – – – – – rapidly, particularly in the – – – – – – countries. How will they be – – – when already in some poor countries many are half-starved?

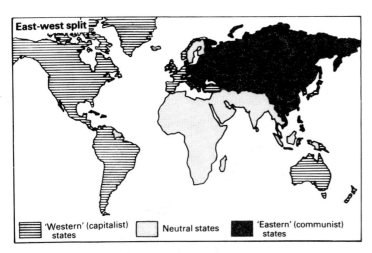

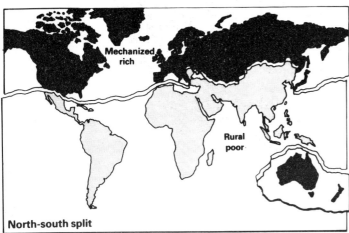

A divided world
These maps show two ways in which the world is seen to be divided. The first shows, very broadly, the division between the capitalist and the communist worlds. The second shows a different division, based broadly on the distribution of wealth in the world.

2 The heads and tails of these sentences have been mixed. Write them out correctly.

(a) Nuclear energy	(1) may lead to more unemployment.
(b) Most richer countries	(2) have higher birth rates.
(c) Private enterprise	(3) believes that land, banks and factories should be run by the state.
(d) Electronic computers	(4) may lead to the end of civilization.
(e) Most poorer countries	(5) have lower birth rates.
(f) Communism	(6) thinks people should be free to make whatever profits they can.

3 *Statements of fact* Write out the four statements in each group in what you think is their order of importance or interest. Say in each group why you decided to put one particular statement first.

(a) The new industrial revolution
 (1) is largely a matter of electronics and physics.
 (2) increases health, leisure and the chance of complete destruction.
 (3) will greatly reduce the amount of drudgery and boredom.
 (4) will enable much clerical work to be done by machines.

(b) Increase in world population
 (1) will lead to a population of six thousand million by the year 2000.
 (2) is creating a big problem of food production and distribution.
 (3) is due largely to falling death rate.
 (4) is more rapid in under-developed countries.

4 *The right order* Write these out in the order of happening.

(a) There was disagreement between Russia and China.
(b) World population will probably be six thousand million.
(c) World population took 100 years to double.

94

Stamp to commemorate an agreed ban on nuclear testing in 1963.

5 *The main idea* Write out the one sentence which tells what you think is the main idea of this topic.

(a) The modern world has many problems which must be solved if civilization is to survive.
(b) The scientific advance may lead to more unemployment and greater risk of starvation.
(c) Solving racial and population problems depends largely upon change in the attitude of the mainly white, prosperous countries.
(d) The peace of the world is endangered by its division into north v south and into east v west.

6 Make a list of the food you eat at breakfast, lunch and tea.

7 Which part of the world do we live in according to the maps on this page?

8 How do you think rich countries can help poor countries?

9 Collect Oxfam or War on Want leaflets and compare the intake of food for children in India with your answer to question 6.

10 Find out which countries have:

(a) the highest birth rate
(b) the highest death rate
(c) the shortest life expectancy
(d) the lowest income
(e) the least industry
(f) the least wealth
(g) the greatest debts

East and west, old and new?

Index

Answers				
1 a	**4** c	**7** b	**10** a	**13** c
2 b	**5** c	**8** b	**11** b	**14** c
3 b	**6** c	**9** c	**12** b	